Personification and the Sublime

STEVEN KNAPP

Personification and
the Sublime ❧
Milton to Coleridge

Harvard University Press
Cambridge, Massachusetts
London, England   1985

Copyright © 1985 by the President and Fellows of Harvard College
All rights reserved
Printed in the United States of America
10 9 8 7 6 5 4 3 2 .1

Publication of this book has been aided by a grant from the
Andrew W. Mellon Foundation.

This book is printed on acid-free paper, and its binding materials
have been chosen for strength and durability.

Library of Congress Cataloging in Publication Data

Knapp, Steven, 1951–
    Personification and the sublime.

    Includes index.
    1. English poetry—History and criticism.
2. Personification in literature. 3. Allegory.
4. Sublime, The, in literature. 5. Milton, John,
1608–1674—Allegory and symbolism. 6. Coleridge,
Samuel Taylor, 1772–1834—Allegory and symbolism.
7. Wordsworth, William, 1770–1850—Allegory and
symbolism. I. Title.
PR508.P35K59 1985   821'.009'15   84-28985
ISBN 0-674-66320-9 (alk. paper)

In memory of Thomas Weiskel

Acknowledgments

My debts to numerous scholars are recorded in the text and notes. Several of those scholars—M. H. Abrams, Harold Bloom, Leslie Brisman, Neil Hertz, and Thomas Weiskel—have also been my teachers and have influenced my thinking in more ways than I can adequately trace or acknowledge. I am grateful to them, and to the friends and colleagues who have helped to refine my arguments: Paul Alpers, Richard Feingold, Frances Ferguson, Joel Fineman, Michael Fried, Catherine Gallagher, Stephen Greenblatt, Walter Benn Michaels, Morton Paley, and Ralph W. Rader.

A portion of Chapter 4 appeared in *Modern Language Notes,* 99 (1984), 1007–1022, and is reprinted by permission of The Johns Hopkins University Press.

Finally, I wish to thank the following for indispensable practical help: Celeste Gnutti, Jeffrey Knapp, and above all, as always, Diane Robinson Knapp.

Contents

Personification and the Sublime

Thus we see how many ways Poetry addresses it self to the Imagination, as it has not only the whole Circle of Nature for its Province, but makes new Worlds of its own, shews us Persons who are not to be found in Being, and represents even the Faculties of the Soul, with her several Virtues and Vices, in a sensible Shape and Character.

Addison, *Spectator*, no. 419, 1712

The Reader will find that personifications of abstract ideas rarely occur in these volumes; and, I hope, are utterly rejected, as an ordinary device to elevate the style, and raise it above prose . . . I have wished to keep my Reader in the company of flesh and blood . . .

Wordsworth, Preface to *Lyrical Ballads*, 1802

Introduction

The impulse behind this study was a suspicion that more was at stake in the transition from eighteenth-century to Romantic accounts of personification than a fondness for abstractions on one side and a distaste for conventional artifice on the other. In itself this suspicion was far from original. Earlier studies by M. H. Abrams and others had long since complicated the textbook scenario of a switch in literary allegiances from allegorical to "symbolic" forms.[1] What had not been sufficiently recognized, it seemed to me, was the persistent and often frank expression of contradictory attitudes toward personification, not only throughout both periods but even within related writings by an individual critic. The most striking instances of this almost systematic ambivalence toward personification were, first, the notorious critical debate over the propriety of Milton's allegory of Sin and Death in *Paradise Lost;* and second, more than rich enough to match a century-long critical controversy, the writings of Coleridge.

An investigation of these examples revealed that critical ambivalence toward personification was symptomatic of a broader ambivalence toward poetic power. Allegorical personification—the endowing of metaphors with the agency of literal persons—was only the most obvious and extravagant instance of what Enlightenment writers perceived, with a mixture of admiration and uneasiness, as the unique ability of poetic genius to give the force of literal reality to figurative "inventions." Once the symptomatic importance of the interest in personification is understood, the seemingly pedantic disputes over Milton's right to indulge in allegory take on a larger and more peculiar meaning. Critics from Joseph Addison onward saw more in Milton's allegory than a violation of neoclassical rules. Milton's Sin and Death struck eighteenth-century readers as "Gothic" intruders in the essentially realistic and classical world of the epic.[2] But more important than the incongruous presence of such agents was their contagious effect on the ostensibly literal agents with which they interacted. The trouble with Milton's power to transform abstract concepts into animated beings was not merely its inherent primitiveness and irrationality, but its *reversibility*. Once the boundaries between literal and figurative agency were erased, it seemed that nothing would prevent the imagination from metaphorizing literal agents as easily as it literalized metaphors. "The impression of real existence, essential to an epic poem," Lord Kames remarked in his *Elements of Criticism,* "is inconsistent with that figurative existence which is essential to an allegory; and therefore no means can more effectively prevent the impression of reality, than to introduce allegorical beings co-operating with those whom we conceive to be really existing."[3] Yet the same "strange jumble of truth and fiction" that disturbed Milton's eighteenth-century audience also won him the highest admiration of readers committed to the aesthetics of the "sublime."

The close relation between personification and the sublime has been recognized often but never adequately explained. Personifications seem to have provided satisfying objects of sublime admiration precisely because of the special features that set them apart from other fictional characters. But just what criteria of the sublime did they appear to fulfill? The wealth of recent commentary on the sublime makes any new argument on the subject difficult to summarize. At this point I can only anticipate the interpretations of Burke and Kant which the reader will find presented at length in Chapter 3. Briefly, the answer appears to lie, once again, in the nature of personified agency, and in the contrast between such agency and the lives of our ordinary selves. For the sublime depends on an ideal of perfect, self-originating agency that no one really expects or wants to fulfill. To "experience" the sublime was not quite, as some historians have argued, to identify oneself with a transcendent ideal of pure subjective power, but rather to entertain that ideal as an abstract, fantastic, unattainable possibility. Kant, along with Burke and the English satirists, was aware of the intriguing proximity of *hypsos* to bathos, of subjective "freedom" to a mad or comical inflation of the self. The sublime, as Kant explains it, is therefore programmatically ambivalent: it demands a simultaneous identification with and dissociation from images of ideal power. Unless the subject in some degree identifies with the ideal, the experience reduces to mere pretense. But total identification collapses the distinction between ideal and empirical agency and leads to a condition of "rational raving" that Kant designated "fanaticism."

As objects of sublime admiration, personifications exemplify—one might almost say they caricature—Kant's scheme in two ways. First, what distinguishes a personification, at least in theory, from other fictional agents is the virtually total saturation of its "personality" by the thematic idea it represents. This amounts to no more than the commonplace observation that a personification derives its appearance and behavior from iconographic emblems of its allegorical content. Milton's Death is dark, shapeless, ravenous, dart-bearing, and possessed, for now, of the tokens of kingship. In theory at least, every feature of such an agent should derive from the conventional signs of what it stands for. In many of the most striking instances of sublime personification, however, the agent's total dependence *on* its idea is matched by a reflexive consciousness *of* its idea: the personification is self-consciously obsessed with the grounds of its own allegorical being. As Coleridge noticed, it becomes the primary "patient" of its own agency. If the personification knows anything at all, it knows itself, with a symmetrical purity unmatched by anything in empirical consciousness.

In their radical self-absorption—one thinks, for instance, of Spenser's at once homicidal and suicidal Despair—allegorical personifications are nearly perfect embodiments of the sublime ideal. But they fit Kant's account in a second way as well. To an eighteenth-century or a Coleridgean reader, their patent fictionality reveals and in a sense enforces the inaccessibility of their self-originating power. This combination of fanatic self-absorption and overt fictionality perfectly matches the dual criteria of the sublime, its conflicting requirements of identification and distance. Indeed, in eighteenth-century poetic practice, the antithetical structure of the sublime experience is sometimes divided between two agents: a personified abstraction, frozen in a posture of fanatic reflexiveness; and an urbanely skeptical speaker, who contemplates the personification as his own allegorical surrogate.[4] It is a subsidiary claim of the following argument—a claim developed in the reading of Collins' "Ode to Fear" (Chapter 3)—that part of the interest of the eighteenth-century sublime ode lies in the tension between these two counterpoised agents.

Condensed as they are, these remarks on the links between personification and the sublime already suggest the impossibility of keeping this study within the boundaries of strictly literary history. And the appearance in the title of Milton and Coleridge further indicates why this should be so. Not only is the period's interest in literary personification symptomatic of a larger interest in poetic power; poetic power turns out to stand for a philosophical, theological, and indeed political interest in a certain ambivalent notion of the self. The critic who above all makes the broader implications of personification inescapable is Coleridge, whose scattered, conflicting, but probing remarks on poetic agency are in one sense the central data this study seeks to explain. Each of the topics alluded to so far makes an appearance somewhere in Coleridge's prose, though often in a strikingly idiosyncratic form. To spend any time looking at a historical phenomenon through Coleridge's eyes is to find oneself committed to a set of oddly specific examples and habits of thought that gradually—if only through insistent repetition—take on increasingly general force. In Coleridge's writings, the widespread ambivalence toward personification acquires at once its most precise and most abstract expression. Allegory, to Coleridge, was both a cause of and an antidote to what he, like Kant, perceived as an attractive but disturbing violence in the relation between ideal agency and empirical consciousness. But Coleridge tended to reject the oscillation between literal and figurative effects, calling instead for a reconciling "medium between *Literal* and *Metaphorical*"—not only in poetry but in all areas of thought.[5]

Partly because of its Coleridgean orientation, then, this book has at least one of the characteristics that have irritated readers of Coleridge himself: a mixture of extreme specificity (in the concentration on a narrow strand of one literary tradition) and grandiose philosophical speculation (in the claims that this tradition exemplifies a broader problem in the period's conception of literature and of the self). The only defense of such a combination is a plea that the literary tradition cannot be understood in a more specifically literary way, while the philosophical issues are uniquely sharpened through their transposition into these particular literary terms. In any event, this combination of interests helps to account for the book's unorthodox structure. In defiance of chronology, I have placed Coleridge first; I could see no alternative to confronting the reader with the full network of interrelated concerns right at the start. The subsequent chapters attempt to unravel this Coleridgean tangle and to pursue a few of its separate threads to their historically distinct origins.

Chapter 2 analyzes the eighteenth-century critical controversy over Milton's Sin and Death. But I postpone an account of Milton's allegorical practice until after Chapters 3 and 4, which explore the theoretical and practical relations between personification and the sublime. Only after the eighteenth-century and Romantic interest in sublime personification is understood does it make sense to return to *Paradise Lost,* this time to determine whether anything in Milton's own attitude toward personification corresponds to the ambivalence his allegory occasioned in later readers. The answer is largely negative. Milton seems not to have shared his successors' interest in the thematic significance of figurative agency as such. This discovery raises a further question, which only a broader study than the present one could attempt to answer: what accounts for the emergence, at the end of the Renaissance, of an interest in figurative language—indeed of poetic fiction in general—as intrinsically meaningful? Readers familiar with the intellectual history of this period will think, appropriately, of Bacon, Locke, and the Royal Society—of the general rise of empiricism and the concomitant ambivalence toward deviations from plain speech. Without challenging this scholarly consensus, I conclude with a brief indication of how it might be modified by a fuller investigation of the problems of belief and agency introduced in this essay.

A few words are in order about the topics and writers this study deliberately ignores. Nothing is said here about the intriguing use of personifications in eighteenth-century descriptions, such as James Thomson's, of natural processes and landscapes; or about the rhetorical value of the semipersonified metaphors that energize Johnson's verse and prose. These modes of personification have been surveyed before, and I have no reason to think that my investigations of sublime personification illuminate them further.[6] At the other end of the scale, I have avoided the fully animated mythic figures of Shelley and Blake. There is some reason to question whether Blake's Zoas or Shelley's pantheon in *Prometheus Unbound* are genuinely allegorical in the eighteenth-century sense. A student of Romantic myth-making like Northrop Frye may or may not be right to insist that "we must not expect to find in Blake any kind of personification, or attempt to give life to an abstraction."[7] But there is another reason that mythopoeic works lie outside the concerns of this book. Much of the interest of the *issue* of personification—apart from its value as a stylistic device—depends on an overt distinction between allegorical and literal agents. In the partly figurative and partly literal characters of Romantic myth-making, the contrast between these separate kinds of agency disappears. I have focused instead on examples in which the shock of encountering embodied metaphors is clearly felt.

The moment we indulge our affections, the earth is metamorphosed: all its tragedies and ennuis vanish, all duties even; nothing remains to fill eternity but two or three persons. But then a person is a *cause*. What is Luther but Protestantism? or Columbus but Columbia? And were I assured of meeting Ellen tomorrow, would it be less than a world, a personal world? Death has no bitterness in the light of that thought.

Emerson, *Journals*, December 14, 1834

1 Coleridge on Allegory and Violence

In a lecture on *Romeo and Juliet* given to the London Philosophical Society on December 9, 1811, Coleridge offers a two-part defense of "what have often been censured as Shakespeare's conceits."[1] His first justification is conventional, even classical: Shakespeare's extravagant figures are usually appropriate to their dramatic speakers; they belong "to the state, age, or feeling of the individual." Coleridge's second argument merely adds historical to dramatic propriety.[2] When the figures "cannot be vindicated" by referring to Shakespeare's characters, "they may well be excused by the taste of his own and of the preceding age." And Coleridge gives an example, ostensibly to illustrate the second principle:

> Here's much to do with hate, but more with love:—
> Why then, O brawling love! O loving hate!
> O anything, of nothing first created!
> O heavy lightness! serious vanity!
> Misshapen chaos of well-seeming forms!
> Feather of lead, bright smoke, cold fire, sick health!
> Still-waking sleep, that is not what it is![3]

In his commentary on the example, Coleridge shifts ground from history to psychology. What *now* matters in Romeo's speech is not the exemplification of Elizabethan taste, but its expression of contradiction and ambivalence. In fact, the example triggers a startling digression, away from Shakespeare, the issue of decorum, and Romeo's metaphysical wit, and into the alien territory of Milton, allegory, and the aesthetics of the sublime. The following remarks, as transcribed by John Payne Collier, come directly after the example from *Romeo:*

> I dare not pronounce such passages as these to be absolutely unnatural, not merely because I consider the author a much better judge than I can be, but because I can understand and allow for an effort of the mind, when it would describe what it cannot satisfy itself with the description of, to reconcile opposites and qualify contradictions, leaving a middle state of mind more strictly appropriate to the imagination than any other, when it is, as it were, hovering between images. As soon as it is fixed on one image, it becomes understanding; but while it is unfixed and wavering between them, attaching itself permanently to none, it is imagination. Such is the fine description of Death in Milton:—
>
> > "The other shape,
> > If shape it might be call'd, that shape had none
> > Distinguishable in member, joint, or limb,
> > Or substance might be call'd, that shadow seem'd,
> > For each seem'd either: black it stood as night;
> > Fierce as ten furies, terrible as hell,
> > And shook a dreadful dart: what seem'd his head
> > The likeness of a kingly crown had on."
> > *Paradise Lost,* Book II [666–673].
>
> The grandest efforts of poetry are where the imagination is called forth, not to produce a distinct form, but a strong working of the mind, still offering what is still repelled, and again creating what is again rejected; the result being what the poet wishes to impress, namely, the substitution of a sublime feeling of the unimaginable for a mere image.

Coleridge goes on to criticize painters who "have attempted pictures of the meeting between Satan and Death at the gates of Hell; and how was Death represented? Not as Milton has described him, but by the most defined thing that can be imagined—a skeleton, the dryest and hardest image that it is possible to discover; which, instead of keeping the mind in a state of activity, reduces it to the merest passivity,—an image, compared with which a square, a triangle, or any other mathematical figure, is a luxuriant fancy."[4]

In a single dense paragraph, Coleridge's elliptical and self-revising argument has taken him from a conventional account of poetic diction to a spirited assault on definite perception. I have quoted the passage at length because it contains the ingredients of much of the argument that follows. It connects the Romantic notion of a "reconciling" imagination with the eighteenth-century theory of the sublime, and it links both of these apparently disparate topics to a controversial episode in *Paradise Lost,* the allegory of Sin and Death. Throughout the eighteenth century, Milton's allegory was controversial, because it was thought to be an irrational intrusion into the realistic clarity and continuity of the epic. By the time it reached Coleridge, Milton's personification virtually carried the issue of allegory as part of its thematic content. The example Coleridge uses to dissociate the imagination from fixed visual perception is thus multiply "negative": by virtue of its oxymoronic style, its association with disruptions of poetic unity, and of course its referent, death. (Even the narrative role of Milton's personification suggests discontinuity and interruption: the figure momentarily halts Satan's quest and threatens to reverse the main epic action before it begins.)

The source of Coleridge's example must be Edmund Burke, who uses precisely the same example from Milton to ground his own claims for "obscurity" as a source of the sublime.[5] Burke shares Coleridge's sense of the inability of painting to match sublime personification: poetry's "apparitions, its chimeras, its harpies, its allegorical figures, are grand and affecting; and though Virgil's Fame, and Homer's Discord, are obscure, they are magnificent figures. These figures in painting would be clear enough, but I fear they might become ridiculous" (*PE,* p. 64). But Burke lacks Coleridge's emphasis on reconciliation or its negative equivalent, oscillation. For Burke, the relation of obscurity to the sublime is far more direct: "It is our ignorance of things that causes all our admiration, and chiefly excites our passions" (*PE,* p. 61). And ignorance gets its power, like all sources of the sublime, from *fear* (*PE,* pp. 57–58, 63). The combination of darkness, ignorance, and fear accounts for the power of Milton's description, in which "all is dark, uncertain, confused, terrible, and sublime to the last degree" (*PE,* p. 59). The reference to confusion is the closest Burke comes to Coleridge's interest in the relations between opposites. Reconciliation belongs, if anywhere in Burke's aesthetic, in the register of the beautiful, not the sublime.

Coleridge's paragraph, then, is puzzling for two reasons. First, it associates a metaphysic and psychology of reconciliation with an aesthetic of terror and discontinuity. Second, it gives prominence to a controversial instance of allegorical personification, despite Coleridge's well-known disparagement of allegory. In what follows I will show why the convergence of these issues— the value of allegorical personification, the violence associated with the sublime, and the reconciling or mediating role of the imagination—is not accidental.[6]

Allegory and Symbol

Remarks on allegory, expressing varying degrees of sympathy and disapproval, are scattered throughout Coleridge's writings.[7] But two discussions—neither one sympathetic to allegory— have provoked continual interpretation by students of Coleridge and of critical theory. The intensity, ingenuity, and sheer quantity of such commentary is strangely disproportionate to the length and purposes of the passages themselves, but they remain the inevitable starting point for any account of Coleridge's attitudes toward allegory.[8]

The earlier and more interesting account appears as a digression in *The Statesman's Manual* (1816), Coleridge's "lay sermon" on the value of the Bible as a guide for political leadership. The later but less complicated discussion appears in notes for a lecture of 1818. It includes a lucid definition of literary allegory:

We may . . . safely define allegoric writing as the employment of one set of agents and images with actions and accompaniments correspondent, so as to convey, while in disguise, either moral qualities or conceptions of the mind that are not in themselves objects of the senses, or other images, agents, actions, fortunes, and circumstances, so that the difference is everywhere presented to the eye or imagination while the likeness is suggested to the mind; and this connectedly so that the parts combine to form a consistent whole.[9]

Coleridge goes on to develop the definition with historical examples of allegory that lead him to a largely negative assessment of its poetic feasibility. What commentary on this passage has not tended to emphasize, however, is the way Coleridge narrows his conception of allegory, while developing it, to the single issue of personification. This focus is by no means determined by the definition itself, which might just as easily have led to a concentration on the nature of allegorical imagery, the form of allegorical actions, or the kinds of "moral qualities or conceptions of the mind" that lend or fail to lend themselves to allegorical treatment. In fact, Coleridge's approach is at first rather general; he begins to list various allegorical types: "picture allegories, or real or supposed pictures interpreted and moralized, and satirical allegories." Of these, he notes, "we have several instances among the classics—as the Tablet of Cebes, the Choice of Hercules, and Simonides' origin of women—but of narrative or epic allegories scarce any, the multiplicity of their gods and goddesses precluding it—unless we choose rather to say that all the machinery of their poets is allegorical." In the course of this characteristically self-revising sentence, Coleridge has switched from a typology of allegorical genres, a natural supplement to his definition, to the problem of epic "machinery," which soon turns into the thorny problem of personification. Allegory is in trouble almost before its history begins, owing to the trickiness of sorting out personifications and gods:

Of a people who raised altars to fever, to sport, to fright, etc., it is impossible to determine how far they meant a personal power or a personification of a power. This only is certain, that

the introduction of these agents could not have the same unmixed effect as the same agents used allegorically produce on
our minds, but something more nearly resembling the effect
produced by the introduction of characteristic saints in the Roman
Catholic poets, or of Moloch, Belial, and Mammon in the second
Book of *Paradise Lost* compared with his Sin and Death.

(*MC*, p. 30)

The "mixed" effects of epic agency will be explored in the
next chapter, on eighteenth-century views of epic allegory, but
here we need only notice that Coleridge's distinction between
classical semipersonifications and purely allegorical agents begins to blur as he proceeds. The distinction is complicated by
the historical claim that "narrative allegory" in its "modern"
form originated in Prudentius' *Psychomachia* as "a substitute for
the mythological imagery of polytheism, and differing from it
only in the more obvious and intentional distinction of the sense
from the symbol, and the known unreality of the latter—so as
to be *a kind of intermediate step between actual persons and mere
personifications*" (*MC*, pp. 30–31; my emphasis).[10] While the
reference to an "intentional distinction of the sense from the
symbol" might seem to confirm the earlier separation between
allegorical agents and the classical pantheon, the end of the
sentence abruptly confers on the agents of narrative allegory
exactly the intermediate or undecidable status earlier given to
the gods. By specifying *narrative* allegory Coleridge presumably
means to exclude the stationary figures of eighteenth-century
"poetic diction," figures whose signifying functions absorb their
personalities, virtually without remainder. But his own earlier
examples of "unmixed" allegory were Milton's virulently active
Sin and Death. Allegory in general thus begins to assume the
intermediate form that will turn out to be its chief poetic liability.[11] From some points of view—including a later one of
Coleridge's—intermediacy might count as a strength. "But for
this very cause," Coleridge announces, narrative allegory

is incapable of exciting any lively interest for any length of time,
for if the allegoric personage be strongly individualized so as to
interest us, we cease to think of it as allegory; and if it does not
interest us, it had better be away. The dullest and most defective

parts of Spenser are those in which we are compelled to think of his agents as allegories—and how far the Sin and Death of Milton are exceptions to this censure, is a delicate problem which I shall attempt to solve in another lecture; but in that admirable allegory, the first Part of *Pilgrim's Progress,* which delights every one, the interest is so great that [in] spite of all the writer's attempts to force the allegoric purpose on the reader's mind by his strange names—Old Stupidity of the Tower of Honesty, etc., etc.—his piety was baffled by his genius, and the Bunyan of Parnassus had the better of Bunyan of the conventicle; and with the same illusion as we read any tale known to be fictitious, as a novel, we go on with his characters as real persons, who had been nicknamed by their neighbors.   (*MC*, p. 31)

The promised "solution" to the problem of Milton's allegory is not available in records of Coleridge's lectures, though a list of "Quotations and Passages referred to" in notes for a lecture of 1819 includes a numerical reference to the first line of Milton's description of Death (*PL,* II.666), along with the words "of allegory, and the difference of Poetry from Painting"; perhaps Coleridge returned to the account of Milton's Death with which I began this chapter.[12] The problem in any case seems more intractable than delicate, if one is to judge from Coleridge's exuberant demolition of Bunyan's allegory. It is hard to see how any allegory could escape the dilemma Coleridge describes; allegorical reference now seems flatly opposed to literary interest. What makes this argument a strange one for Coleridge is the way it turns against his familiar ideal of a reconciling medium by locating the weakness of allegory precisely in its intermediate state. And the strangeness becomes acute when this passage is compared to the one in the *Statesman's Manual,* in which allegory is associated with the loss of an intermediate discourse. This time the text in question is not Bunyan but the Bible. Coleridge is deploring the evisceration of scriptural substance by Socinian interpreters. He is led into this polemic against allegorical reading by his claims for the Bible's supreme "applicability to the changes and fortunes of empires":

And in nothing is Scriptural history more strongly contrasted with the histories of highest note in the present age than in its freedom from the hollowness of abstractions. While the latter present a shadow-fight of Things and Quantities, the former gives us the history of Men . . . How should it be otherwise? The histories and political economy of the present and preceding century partake in the general contagion of its mechanic philosophy, and are the *product* of an unenlivened generalizing Understanding. In the Scriptures they are the living *educts* of the Imagination; of that reconciling and mediatory power, which incorporating the Reason in Images of the Sense, and organizing (as it were) the flux of the Senses by the permanence and self-circling energies of the Reason, gives birth to a system of symbols, harmonious in themselves, and consubstantial with the truths, of which they are the *conductors*.[13]

Scriptural "symbols" derive this special substantiality from a doubleness of reference oddly similar to that of narrative allegory as defined in the lecture notes: "In the Scriptures . . . both Facts and Persons must of necessity have a two-fold significance, a past and a future, a temporary and a perpetual, a particular and a universal application. They must be at once Portraits and Ideals." Yet this apparent translation of biblical symbols into what seems to be a perfect exemplification of allegory sets off an extraordinary protest against allegory as a mechanical negation of symbolic life:

> Eheu! paupertina philosophia in paupertinam religionem ducit:—A hunger-bitten and idea-less philosophy naturally produces a starveling and comfortless religion. It is among the miseries of the present age that it recognizes no medium between *Literal* and *Metaphorical*. Faith is either to be buried in the dead letter, or its name and honors usurped by a counterfeit product of the mechanical understanding, which in the blindness of self-complacency confounds SYMBOLS with ALLEGORIES.
>
> (*LS*, p. 30)

The dead letter, standing for biblical fundamentalism, merits only a word of reproach; the excessive and curiously moralizing rhetoric—the charges of usurpation, counterfeiting, and blind self-complacency—is reserved not just for allegory but for the failure to distinguish one kind of double reference from another. Here the pitch of indignation is high enough to sustain

Coleridge's fullest effort to recover the distinction modern discourse has lost:

> Now an Allegory is but a translation of abstract notions into a picture-language which is itself nothing but an abstraction from objects of the senses; the principal being more worthless even than its phantom proxy, both alike unsubstantial, and the former shapeless to boot. On the other hand, a Symbol . . . is characterized by a translucence of the Special in the Individual or of the General in the Especial or of the Universal in the General. Above all by the translucence of the Eternal through and in the Temporal.

The representational instrument of such "translucence" seems oddly like the rhetorical figure of synecdoche. The symbol "always partakes of the Reality which it renders intelligible; and while it enunciates the whole, abides itself as a living part in that Unity, of which it is the representative. The other are but empty echoes which the fancy arbitrarily associates with apparitions of matter, less beautiful but not less shadowy than the sloping orchard or hill-side pasture-field seen in the transparent lake below" (*LS*, pp. 30–31).

By now the dilemma of allegory is clear. Conceived (in Coleridge's lecture notes) as a medium between literal opacity and figurative reference, allegory can fail in two ways: by surrendering its literal power and thus its interest, or by surrendering its figurative content and thus its character as allegory. Or, conceived (in the *Statesman's Manual*) as pure figuration, allegory denies or thwarts the genuine mediation of symbolic translucence. In the latter account, allegory stands for the *absence* of a medium; in the former, it reveals the *impossibility* of the medium it professes to be. The choice between these two equally devastating ways of disparaging allegory seems to depend on context.[14] When criticizing allegory by itself, Coleridge relies on the implausibility of a medium between the literal and the metaphorical; when exalting the intermediacy of scriptural representation, he simply drains allegory of all its mediating claims. The almost irresistible inference to draw from these contradictory maneuvers is that no genuine "medium" in fact exists. And just that inference has been drawn, on various grounds, in the most penetrating recent criticism of Coleridge's distinction.[15] Starting from assumptions that language is essentially arbitrary, mechanical, insubstantial, and "temporal," such criticism suggests that Coleridge appealed to a rather sentimental, quasi-theological notion of the symbol in order to conceal the phenomenological and linguistic truth revealed by allegory.[16] But one can agree that Coleridge's distinction is unstable without at the same time agreeing that such instability shows the primacy of arbitrary figures. It is not clear, for example, why the apparent collapse of a medium between metaphor and literalness necessarily favors metaphor. The key to an alternative interpretation of the Coleridgean medium lies in the nature of symbolic synecdoche, too easily dismissed as a willfully privileged figure of speech.[17]

The impression of willfulness partly results from Coleridge's strange and apparently tendentious language of substance: symbols are "consubstantial with the truths, of which they are *conductors.*" To Paul de Man, for example, the error implicit in this notion of consubstantial representation becomes evident when Coleridge shifts to the metaphor of "translucence," which seems to give up the "material richness" or "material substantiality" that was originally at stake in Coleridge's attack on "the essential thinness of allegory."[18] Yet the adjective "material" is added by de Man. Instead of exposing a naive wish to escape temporality, the fact that Coleridge seems equally comfortable with the metaphors of substance and of translucence suggests that an emphasis on the symbol's materiality is misplaced. A sympathetic account of Coleridge's notion might begin by questioning both the nominalist interpretation of synecdoche and the materialist interpretation of substance. As the context of Coleridge's explanation already implies, and as his own examples of the "medium" will confirm, what is at issue in the promotion of the symbol is not the metaphysical status of representation but the practical consequences of action and belief. What Coleridge presents as a medium between nominal figuration and substantial identity is in fact a distinct alternative to both.

Coleridge's extensive marginalia on the seventeenth-century divine Jeremy Taylor include a note on the symbolic status of the Eucharist. The note is especially helpful because it adopts, with slight but revealing alterations, virtually the same language as the passage in the *Statesman's Manual*. This time—in a shift of historical grounds that is itself illuminating—the agents of error are not the twin extremes of modern Protestantism, fundamentalism and Socinianism, but the more massive opposites of Roman Catholicism and Protestantism in general: "The error on both sides, Roman and Protestant, originates in the confusion of sign or figure with symbol, which latter is always an essential part of that, of the whole of which it is the representative. Not seeing this, and therefore seeing no *medium* between the whole thing and the mere metaphor of the thing, the Romanists took the former or positive pole of error, the Protestants the latter or negative pole." The category of metaphor is now represented by "sign or figure" instead of "allegory"; the casual adjustment of terminology makes it clear that Coleridge treats allegory itself mainly as a synecdoche for nominalism in general, rather than as a specifically literary mode. But the crucial question raised by this passage so far is what Coleridge means by "thing," the "whole thing" the symbol partially represents. The referent which the symbol both inhabits and displays is neither a nominal class nor a substance, but a world of expectations, practices, and acts: "The Eucharist is a symbolic, or solemnizing and *totum in parte* acting of an act, which in a true member of Christ's body is supposed to be perpetual. Thus the husband and wife exercise the duties of their marriage contract of love, protection, obedience, and the like, all the year long, yet solemnize it by a more deliberate and reflecting act of the same love on the anniversary of their marriage."[19]

In offering the ordinary and unmysterious example of a wedding anniversary, which stands for the obligations of marriage at the same time that it partly fulfills them, Coleridge is not retreating from his claims for symbolic consubstantiality; he is showing what he means by "substance."[20] Nor is he demystifying or secularizing the Eucharist by converting the metaphysical claims of transubstantiation into the communicant's act of self-identification with Christ. For Coleridge, real, organic membership in the body of Christ simply *is* the (supposed) perpetual act of participating in that body. Coleridge has thus shifted the locus of consubstantiality from the equation of bread and body to the synecdochic relation between act and history—in this case, between the celebration of the Eucharist and the totality of the believer's practical relations to Christ. Although the example is theological, and the history in question frankly supernatural, what makes the symbolic equation "essential" instead of arbitrary is the impossibility of separating *any* history from the acts that embody it.[21]

Coleridge's substitution of practical participation for the formal criteria of metaphysical identity accounts for the initial strangeness of many of his examples, some of which seem remote from synecdoche. Two such examples of "symbol" appear in an appendix to the *Statesman's Manual* on the difference between Reason—"the knowledge of the laws of the WHOLE considered as ONE"—and Understanding, "which concerns itself exclusively with the quantities, qualities, and relations of *particulars* in time and space" (*LS,* p. 59). The apparent metaphysical gulf between these faculties is bridged, we recall, by the Imagination, which "gives birth" to symbols by "incorporating the Reason in Images of the Sense" (*LS,* p. 29). A science governed, through Imagination, by Reason is thus a science of symbols: "True natural philosophy is comprized in the study of the science and language of *symbols.* The power delegated to nature is all in every part: and by a symbol I mean, not a metaphor or allegory or any other figure of speech or form of fancy, but an actual and essential part of that, the whole of which it represents. Thus our Lord speaks symbolically when he says that 'the eye is the light of the body' " (*LS,* p. 79). Despite the explicit repudiation of metaphor, the example is likely to seem analogical rather than synecdochic.[22] The eye is to the body as a candle is to exterior space; when the candle is hidden the room is dark; when the eye is evil, the body "also is full of darkness" (Luke 11:33–36; Matthew 6:22–23 also gives the "symbol" Coleridge quotes, but not the explicit analogy of the candle). Yet Coleridge elsewhere treats analogy itself as a mode of symbol, not metaphor. His account of symbolic analogy, in the *Aids to Reflection,* is part of a long elaboration of an aphorism on "the tenets peculiar to Christianity" (*CWC,* I, 229–236). After advancing among other things the almost Wittgensteinian claim that "Christianity is not a theory, or a speculation; but a life;—not a philosophy of life, but a life and a living process" (*CWC,* I, 233), Coleridge turns to consider "the language of the Gospel." He begins his exposition by supplanting the opposition between symbol and allegory with a new "distinction between analogous and metaphorical language." Coleridge first ascribes analogy's substantive force to its special relation to belief:

> Analogies are used in aid of conviction: metaphors, as means of illustration. The language is analogous, wherever a thing, power, or principle in a higher dignity is expressed by the same thing, power, or principle in a lower but more known form. Such, for instance, is the language of *John* iii.6. *That which is born of the flesh, is flesh; that which is born of the Spirit, is Spirit.* The latter half of the verse contains the fact asserted; the former half the analogous fact, by which it is rendered intelligible.

He then appeals to the traditional doctrine of accommodation as applied to the anthropomorphic attributes of God:[23]

> If any man choose to call this metaphorical or figurative, I ask him whether with Hobbes and Bolingbroke he applies the same rule to the moral attributes of the Deity? Whether he regards the divine justice, for instance, as a metaphorical term, a mere figure of speech? If he disclaims this, then I answer, neither do I regard the phrase *born again* . . . as a figure or metaphor. I have only to add, that these analogies are the material, or (to speak chemically) the base, of symbols and symbolical expressions; the nature of which is always tautegorical, that is, expressing the same subject but with a difference, in contra-distinction from metaphors and similitudes, which are always allegorical, that is, expressing a different subject but with a resemblance.[24]
> (*CWC,* I, 235)

As the passage makes clear, analogy is not for Coleridge an alternative to the account of symbol as synecdochic; analogy already is synecdoche, by virtue of the common agency on which the analogous terms depend. What makes natural birth more than a figure for spiritual regeneration is the (theological) necessity of attributing both to a single power. Analogous objects are effects of a single cause. Yet for Coleridge substance *is* causality or, in its transcendent designation, "act."[25] Identity of cause thus begins to look like identity of substance. Analogy takes on literal force. And in fact, in the paragraph following the last quotation, Coleridge implicitly equates analogy and literal identity when he warns against the superstitious consequences of "a confusion of metaphor with analogy, and of figurative with literal" (*CWC,* I, 236).

But the progressive literalization of analogy is more than a slip in a typically hasty argument. The symbolic "medium" is generated by just such a "tautegorical" movement from figurative difference toward literal identity—from allegory toward tautology, as the neologism suggests. The second example of "symbol" from the appendix to the *Statesman's Manual* is itself a symbol, a splendid enactment of the tautegorical process it reveals. The passage concerns the "reading" of Nature, which, like the Bible, has both its literal and its figurative sense: "That in its obvious sense and literal interpretation it declares the being and attributes of the Almighty Father, none but the *fool in heart* has ever dared gainsay. But . . . it is the *poetry* of all human nature, to read it likewise in a figurative sense, and to find therein correspondencies [*sic*] and symbols of the spiritual world" (*LS,* p. 70). The abrupt turn from "figurative sense" to "symbols" is already somewhat surprising, since symbols were earlier neither figurative nor literal. As the passage unfolds, literal and figurative effects continue to converge. For an example of the mode of reading he proposes, Coleridge takes as his "chapter" "the flowery meadow" that he claims to contemplate at the moment of writing. The process of symbolization is visible in the "vegetable creation" of the landscape itself, where the harmonizing of arbitrary differences offers a moral lesson to the human agent:

> It seems as if the soul said to herself: from this state hast *thou* fallen! Such shouldst thou still become, thy Self all permeable to a holier power! thy Self at once hidden and glorified by its own transparency, as the accidental and dividuous in this quiet and harmonious object is subjected to the life and light of nature

which shines in it, even as the transmitted power, love and
wisdom, of God over all fills, and shines through, nature! But
what the plant *is*—by an act not its own and unconsiously—*that*
must thou *make* thyself to *become!*   (*LS*, p. 71)

For all its earnestness, the analogy sustains an oscillating play
of identity and difference: the soul speaks to herself, but only
through the landscape and only of her own alienation from that
same harmonious medium of her speech. The plantlife derives
its symbolic identity with the soul from a multiple analogy: it
is "subjected to the life and light of nature," just as nature, like
the soul, is subject to the power and life of God. Yet this identity
is also crossed by a difference, since the moral Self of the soul
is in fact *not* permeated by the "holier power," although it should
be—and yet it can be—only through a most unplantlike active
subjection of itself.

Against the background of this complex analogical counter-
point, Coleridge now moves still closer to tautology by converting the landscape into a symbol of Reason, the governor of
Imagination and the original agent of the conceptual totalities
on which symbolic analogy depends:

> But further, and with particular reference to that undivided
> Reason, neither merely speculative or merely practical, but both
> in one, which I have in this annotation endeavored to contra-
> distinguish from the Understanding, I seem to myself to behold
> in the quiet objects, on which I am gazing, more than an arbitrary
> illustration, more than a mere *simile,* the work of my own Fancy!
> I feel an awe, as if there were before my eyes the same Power,
> as that of the REASON—the same Power working in a lower
> dignity, and therefore a symbol established in the truth of things.
> I feel it alike, whether I contemplate a single tree or flower, or
> meditate on vegetation throughout the world, as one of the great
> organs of the life of nature.   (*LS*, p. 72)

The passage goes on to develop the analogy in a remarkable
incantatory description of plant physiology.[26] As Reason traces
its own self-representation, the collapsing of symbol into sheer
tautology seems complete; Coleridge seems to have shifted from
the partial identities and differences of analogy to the perfect
symmetry of a pure self-recognition. But the passage stops short

of such totalizing identification, which would push it beyond the mode of symbol to the brink of megalomania or bathos. What keeps the passage in the intermediate mode of symbol is the way it blocks the full participation of the self. "I *seem* to myself to behold"—not myself, but Reason. I see my Reason represent itself; yet Reason is not in fact "my own"—*Fancy* is. Reason appears to the self only in what looks to the self like Reason's self-representation. Reason, as Coleridge has noted several pages earlier, both contains and permeates the "regenerated man," but it is not at the same time, like Fancy, empirically present to the self: "It cannot in strict language be called a faculty, much less a personal property, of any human mind! He, with whom it is present, can as little appropriate it, whether totally or by partition, as he can claim ownership in the breathing air or make an enclosure in the cope of heaven" (*LS*, p. 70).

The danger of such appropriation, collapsing the difference between normative truth and the empirical self, produces a need for the partial identity of the symbolic medium, and explains why that medium must be insulated from the total or "literal" identity to which it tends. Once the criteria of real identity are located in the practical world of interpenetrating agencies or "powers," the differences between effects of identical causes are likely to disappear. Instead of a genuine medium between two independent modes of representation, the symbol thus becomes an unstable means of transition from difference to identity. No formal safeguard can prevent the symbol from lapsing once again into the impotence of allegory, by losing its hold on the reality of its object; or from hardening into the "superstition" of literal identity, by appropriating all that reality to itself. In the *Statesman's Manual* the emphasis falls on the former danger—the danger of allegory—because the book's purpose is to establish the practical authority of Scripture. And in fact, the first and obvious target throughout Coleridge's writings tends to be the atomizing formalism of empiricist thought. But there is much in Coleridge to suggest that the deeper and more persistent danger lies in identity—that the symbol must be saved by allegory from its innate gravitation toward the literal.

Even in the context of biblical apologetics the danger of

literalism can outweigh the risk of figurative hollowness. In his posthumous *Confessions of an Inquiring Spirit,* for instance, Coleridge deplores the "literal rendering" of figures as a "still greater evil"—an evil "less attributable to the visionary humor and weak judgment of the individual expositors"—than "the arbitrary allegories and mystic expansions of proper names" (*CWC,* V, 599). In the *Aids to Reflection,* as well as rejecting allegory, Coleridge attacks what he calls the "impropriation" of metaphor, "that is, the taking it literally," which converts the Pauline metaphors of redemption into the harsh anthropomorphic doctrines of "satisfaction," "sacrifice," and "ransom." Even the "consubstantiality" of the sacraments, the precondition of their symbolic status, threatens to harden into fatal identity. Coleridge reminds an imaginary Baptist interlocutor "that a ceremony duly instituted is a chain of gold around the neck of faith; but if in the wish to make it co-essential and consubstantial, you draw it closer and closer, it may strangle the faith it was meant to deck and designate" (*CWC,* I, 338–339).

But these warnings against excessive theological literalism may give an impression of perfunctory fairness, as if their only purpose was to fill out the already too schematic logic of the "medium": having scolded one kind of extremism, Coleridge dutifully turns to the other. The air of complacency is a persistent liability of the Anglican via media, with its traditional condescension toward extremists on either side. A more interesting and less predictable response to the dangers of the literal appears in Coleridge's treatment of poetic agency, where the issue is not just the preservation of the medium, but its production.

Genius and Violence

The issues of allegory and poetic genius were linked in Coleridge's mind as early as 1802, when he included a critique of allegory that anticipated his later attack in a well-known letter to William Sotheby. The letter has won a place in the canon of Romantic manifestos because it marks Coleridge's decisive rejection of his early poetic model, William Lisle Bowles. In the appendix to the *Statesman's Manual*, the perception of vegetation as a symbol of reason is "more than an arbitrary illustration, more than a mere *simile,* the work of my own Fancy!" (*LS,* p. 72). The same attribution of simile to fancy, not imagination, stands behind Coleridge's earlier critique of Bowles. The initial target is Bowles's "perpetual trick of *moralizing* every thing—which is very well, occasionally—but never to see or describe an interesting appearance in nature, without connecting it by dim analogies with the moral world, proves faintness of Impression." The failure to give Nature her due is a sin against the *"one Life"* that presumably guarantees the moral interest of vivid impressions even in the absence of overt moralizing. To Bowles's dim and arbitrary analogies Coleridge opposes imaginative fusion: "A Poet's *Heart* & *Intellect* should be *combined, intimately* combined & *unified,* with the great appearances in Nature—& not merely held in solution & loose mixture with them, in the shape of formal Similies. I do not mean to *exclude* these formal Similies—there are moods of mind, in which they are natural—pleasing moods of mind, & such as a Poet will often have, & sometimes express; but they are not his highest, & most appropriate moods."[27] The relation between "formal Similies" and allegory becomes clear when Coleridge expands this distinction between Bowlesian moralizing and true poetic genius into a contrast between Greek and Hebrew poetry. The point of contrast, anticipating the lecture notes on allegory and polytheism, is the status, in each tradition, of religious personification:

> It must occur to every Reader that the Greeks in their religious poems address always the Numina Loci, the Genii, the Dryads, the Naiads, &c &c—All natural Objects were *dead*—mere hollow Statues—but there was a Godkin or Goddessling *included* in each—In the Hebrew Poetry you find nothing of this poor Stuff—as poor in genuine Imagination, as it is mean in Intellect—/ At best, it is but Fancy, or the aggregating Faculty of the mind—not *Imagination,* or the *modifying,* and *co-adunating* Faculty. This the Hebrew Poets appear to me to have possessed beyond all others—& next to them the English. In the Hebrew Poets each Thing has a Life of it's own, & yet they are all one Life.[28]

The parallel between these remarks and Coleridge's later criticisms of allegory is unmistakable; Bowles, along with the Greeks, is cast in the role later played by Socinian interpreters of Scripture. Between the attacks on Bowles's formal similes and the hollow personifications of Greek religious poetry, however, Coleridge provides an intriguing psychological explanation of Bowles's imaginative failure. His account is somewhat contradictory; we are left uncertain whether Bowles suffers from a congenital defect in his emotional makeup or, more suggestively, from a fear of the sort of power Coleridge imputes to authentic genius: "The truth is—Bowles has indeed the *sensibility* of a poet; but he has not the *Passion* of a great Poet. His latter Writings all want *native* Passion—Milton here & there supplies him with an appearance of it—but he has no native Passion, because he is not a Thinker—& has probably weakened his Intellect by *the haunting Fear of becoming extravagant*."[29]

The view that writers during the Enlightenment ironically crippled their intellects through a fear of extravagant passion was one of which the Romantics were inordinately fond. The fear of extravagance after all inspired some of Swift's and Johnson's most passionate prose. And there is a good deal of evidence that Coleridge was haunted by precisely the same fear. In Coleridge, as in the eighteenth-century writers, the fear of extravagance is partly the symptom of a psychologically genuine ambivalence, and partly an instrument of political, aesthetic, and religious polemic. Both the ambivalence and its polemical function are visible in Coleridge's defense of poetic genius in the second chapter of the *Biographia Literaria*.

Coleridge begins the chapter by announcing his intention "to analyze, and bring forward into distinct consciousness, that complex feeling, with which readers in general take part against the author, in favor of the critic; and the readiness with which they apply to *all* poets the old sarcasm of Horace upon the scribblers of his time: 'Genus irritabile vatum' " (*BL,* I, 30). This opening sentence already suggests the line of Coleridge's defense: he will insist, as usual, on a distinction, this time between the poets of true genius and the irritable scribblers to whom Horace's charge legitimately applies. The distinction was of course thoroughly conventional, and had long ago received its most dazzling English elaboration in Pope's *Epistle to Dr. Arbuthnot*. But, in a characteristically elusive series of substitutions, Coleridge very quickly supplants this binary opposition of poet and scribbler with a more unwieldy ternary scheme. His first and crucial move is to turn scribblers into fanatics:

> A debility and dimness of imaginative power, and a consequent necessity of reliance on the immediate impressions of the senses, do, we well know, render the mind liable to superstition and fanaticism. Having a deficient portion of internal and proper warmth, minds of this class seek in the crowd *circum fana* for a warmth in common, which they do not possess singly . . . Hence the German word for fanaticism (such at least was the original import) is derived from the swarming of bees, namely, Schwär-men, Schwärmerey. The passion being in an inverse proportion to the insight, *that* the more vivid, as *this* the less distinct; anger is the inevitable consequence.[30]   (*BL*, I, 30–31)

Then, in what seems to be a completion of the binary scheme, Coleridge adds the following description, apparently an account of true genius: "But where the ideas are vivid, and there exists an endless power of combining and modifying them, the feelings and affections blend more easily and intimately with these ideal creations, than with the objects of the senses; the mind is affected by thoughts, rather than by things; and only then feels the requisite interest even for the most important events, and accidents, when by means of meditation they have passed into *thoughts*" (*BL*, I, 31). But, as the very next sentence reveals, this portrait of self-sustaining imaginative power is not yet the ideal of genius that Coleridge would oppose to fanatic scribbling. Instead, he now has in mind a triple distinction. The proper ideal is not this polar opposite to fanaticism, but rather the medium between these two opposite extremes: "The sanity of the mind is between superstition with fanaticism on the one hand; and enthusiasm with indifference and a diseased slowness to action on the other."

Readers familiar with eighteenth-century doublets will recognize what has happened here; the reference to fanaticism has more or less automatically suggested its twin extravagance, enthusiasm. Yet no sooner is the opposition established, along with the inevitable Coleridgean call for its medium, than this whole scheme collapses into a new opposition, this time no longer between scribbling and genius, but between two modes of genius itself. Fanaticism and enthusiasm, after being excluded from Coleridge's conception of genius, are now reproduced *within* that conception, respectively as its active and contemplative—or malignant and benign—modes. I repeat the sentence on the need for a medium in order to make clear how that medium turns into an oscillation between the two extremes it excludes:

> The sanity of the mind is between superstition with fanaticism on the one hand; and enthusiasm with indifference and a diseased slowness to action on the other. For the conceptions of the mind may be so vivid and adequate, as to preclude that impulse to the realizing of them, which is strongest and most restless in those, who possess more than mere *talent* (or the faculty of appropriating and applying the knowledge of others) yet still want something of the creative, and self-sufficing power of absolute *Genius*. For this reason therefore, they are men of *commanding* genius. While the former rest content between thought and reality, as it were in an intermundium of which their own living spirit supplies the *substance,* and their imagination the ever-varying *form;* the latter must impress their preconceptions on the world without, in order to present them back to their own view with the satisfying degree of clearness, distinctness, and individuality.   (*BL,* I, 31–32)

Like the fanatic, the commanding genius, for all his genuine energy, is still forced by a degree of inner poverty to depend on the external confirmation of his powers. The absolute genius is wholly absorbed and sustained by intellect, but for that very reason one wonders why he, any more than the enthusiast, should be driven to produce at all. Yet the absolute genius is hardly the figure of Hamlet-like self-involvement and impotence that the description of enthusiasm seems to suggest.[31] Coleridge's examples of the serenity of absolute genius are Chaucer, Shakespeare, Spenser, and even Milton (*BL,* I, 33–37). While absolute genius is the heir, in Coleridge's paragraph, to the virtual solipsism of enthusiasm, it also serves as the sane medium between enthusiasm and fanaticism; its association with the medium is perhaps captured in the strange term "intermundium." The fact that absolute genius stands both for the medium and for one of the extremes shows how precarious is the balance Coleridge's ideal requires. The impression of intellectual conceptions on the external world is after all the legitimate function of the imagination, which produces symbols, once again, precisely by "incorporating the Reason in Images of the Sense" (*LS,* p. 29). In short, it is hard to see how genius could operate without the powers—and the liabilities—of both the absolute and the commanding modes. But the reason Coleridge insists on the distinction is not far to seek; he wants to dissociate genius from its historical implication in violence. The whole category of the commanding genius is intended to absorb the violence that the "complex feeling" of "readers in general" is all too ready to impute to genius per se. As poets of action, commanding geniuses, Coleridge goes on,

> in tranquil times are formed to exhibit a perfect poem in palace or temple or landscape-garden; or a tale of romance in canals that join sea with sea, or in walls of rock, which shouldering back the billows imitate the power, and supply the benevolence of nature to sheltered navies; or in aqueducts that arching the wide vale from mountain to mountain give a Palmyra to the desert. But alas! in times of tumult they are the men destined to come forth as the shaping spirit of Ruin, to destroy the wisdom of ages in order to substitute the fancies of a day, and to change kings and kingdoms, as the wind shifts and shapes the clouds. (*BL,* I, 32–33)

By an identification of style, theme, and agency thoroughly typical of the sublime, the agents of sublime violence are here condensed into the kind of figure we will meet repeatedly in subsequent chapters, the sublime personification. The passage achieves its somewhat grandiloquent power by indulging in a rhetorical version of the literal violence it deplores.

The split in Coleridge's conception between the potentially fanatical genius of external action and the enthusiastic genius of aesthetic creation reappears elsewhere, sometimes as a distinction between opposite types of poetic genius, sometimes as an oscillating tendency in all genius as such. Later in the same chapter of the *Biographia,* for example, Coleridge takes up in a footnote the alleged proximity of genius to madness:

> This is one instance among many of deception, by the telling the half of a fact, and omitting the other half, when it is from their mutual counteraction and neutralization, that the *whole* truth arises, as a tertium aliquid different from either. Thus in Dryden's famous line "Great wit" (which here means genius) "to madness sure is near allied." Now as far as the profound sensibility, which is doubtless *one* of the components of genius, were alone considered single and unbalanced, it might be fairly described as exposing the individual to a greater chance of mental derangement; but then a more than usual rapidity of association, a more than usual power of passing from thought to thought, and image to image, is a component equally essential; and in the due modification of each by the other the GENIUS itself consists; so that it would be as just as fair to describe the earth, as in imminent danger of exorbitating, or of falling into the sun, according as the assertor of the absurdity *confined* his attention either to the projectile or to the attractive force exclusively.[32]   (*BL,* I, 44)

The "more than usual rapidity of association" implies that what saves the genius from madness is not the strength of his imagination but his fancy. According to Coleridge's most famous definition, fancy, unlike either primary or secondary imagination, "is indeed no other than a mode of Memory emancipated from the order of time and space"; it "must receive all its materials ready made from the law of association." "The primary IMAGINATION" is "the living Power and prime Agent of all human Perception, and as a repetition in the finite mind of the eternal act of creation in the infinite I AM." Somewhere between the divine but impersonal agency of primary perception and the passive mechanism of associative fancy, Coleridge locates the "secondary" Imagination, which "co-exist[s] with the conscious will": "It dissolves, diffuses, dissipates, in order to re-create; or where this process is rendered impossible, yet still at all events it struggles to idealize and to unify" (*BL,* I, 304–305). Everyone who writes about Coleridge has something to say about the sense, sources, or ambiguities of Coleridge's hasty and unargued distinction of faculties. I cite the passage here only to show how closely it parallels the footnote on genius. The secondary imagination clearly matches the *tertium aliquid* of creative sanity. In its struggle to idealize and unify, the secondary imagination reflects the concentrating or, in Coleridge's gravitational simile, the "attractive" force of genius; in its dissolving, diffusing, dissipating action it suggests the "projectile" force of rapid association and substitution. And the same dangers might be said to attend both of these versions of the Coleridgean medium. Like genius, the secondary imagination threatens to lapse into the eccentric inconsequence of fancy, sliding pointlessly from image to image. But without such tendencies of differentiation it would be indistinguishable from primary imagination; the "conscious will" would lose itself in a mad identification of imaginary recreation with involuntary perceptual fact. Just as the symbol needed to be saved from literal identity by the persistence of allegorical difference, so the imagination must be saved by fancy from its own potential violence.

Coleridge sometimes uses the same metaphors of centripetal and centrifugal force to account for differences between individual geniuses.[33] The most striking case is his frequent comparison of Shakespeare with Milton. Thus Shakespeare occupies "one of the two glory-smitten summits of the poetic mountain, with Milton as his compeer not rival. While the former darts himself forth, and passes into all the forms of human character and passion, the one Proteus of the fire and the flood; the other attracts all forms and things to himself, into the unity of his own IDEAL. All things and modes of action shape themselves anew in the being of MILTON; while SHAKESPEARE becomes all things, yet for ever remaining himself" (*BL,* II, 27–28).[34]

The same comparison reappears in a later manuscript (dated "Sept. 18, 1820") as an opposition between Milton's objectification of poetry and Shakespeare's poeticization of reality. This time the comparison takes place in a difficult passage on the nature of objectivity, which Coleridge defines as the "identity of Truth and Fact." By "truth" here Coleridge apparently means universal agreement, which he conceives as a kind of collective subjectivity: "as when A *sees*, and Millions *see* . . . and the Seeing of the millions is what constitutes to A & to each of the millions the *objectivity* of the sight, the *equivalent* of a Common Object." By "fact" he means "a proper external Object." Without transition this definition of objectivity leads to the claim "that Milton hid the Poetry in or *transformed* (not transubstantiated) the Poetry into the objectivity while Shakespeare, in all things, the divine opposite, or antithetic Correspondent of the divine Milton, transformed the *Objectivity* into *Poetry*." The combination of poetry and objectivity gives both poets "the same *weight* of effect," but for different reasons: if Shakespeare's power lies in "the exceeding *felicity* (subjectivity)" of his characters, the weightiness of Milton's characters derives from their "exceeding *propriety*."[35] The difference, as Coleridge reveals in still later comments, depends on the location of "subjectivity" in the works of each poet. Homer lacks subjectivity altogether; but Milton and Shakespeare have it in different ways: "There is a subjectivity of the poet, as of Milton, who is himself before himself in every thing he writes; and there is a subjectivity of the *persona*, or dramatic character, as in all Shakespeare's great creations, Hamlet, Lear, &c." Similarly, "Shakespeare's poetry is characterless; that is, it does not reflect the individual Shakespeare; but John Milton is himself in every line of the Paradise Lost."[36] Milton's characters, "his Satan, his Adam, his Raphael, almost his Eve—are all John Milton." Yet such centripetal egotism is not for Coleridge a sign of fanatical appropriation. On the contrary, the "sense of this intense egotism" is what gives Coleridge "the greatest pleasure in reading Milton's works. The egotism of such a man is a revelation of spirit."[37]

Though opposites, Shakespeare and Milton thus remain ideal expressions of the secondary imagination in its highest manifestation, poetic genius. In their complementary tendencies of poeticizing diffusion and literalizing concentration, they separately personify the antithetical requirements of the Coleridgean medium. Yet the instability of that medium is at least implied in the morally paradoxical endorsement of Miltonic "egotism." The instability becomes explicit, however, when

Coleridge tries to present his own genius in the same antithetical terms. In the *Aids to Reflection* he quotes the anticipated mockery of an imaginary reviewer, who will relegate "the compiler" of the *Aids* to the enthusiastic—fanatical?—sect of Swift's Aeolists,

> whose fruitful imaginations led them into certain notions, which although in appearance very unaccountable, are not without their mysteries and their meanings: furnishing plenty of matter for such, whose converting imaginations dispose them to reduce all things into types; who can make shadows, no thanks to the sun; and then mould them into substances, no thanks to philosophy; whose peculiar talent lies in fixing tropes and allegories to the letter, and refining what is literal into figure and mystery.   (*CWC*, I, 155)

Here the self-mockery is sufficiently gentle and attractive to dissociate the passage from the scatological violence directed against the original Aeolists in Swift's *Tale of a Tub*. A stronger version of Coleridge's poetic ambivalence emerges when the issue is not his eccentricity but his own relation to literary violence; when the objects alternately reduced to types and molded into substances are not merely things and shadows, but persons; when what is at stake in the relation between imagination and allegory is precisely "the sacred distinction between things and persons" (*BL*, I, 205).[38]

Violence and Personification

Sometime in the spring of 1803 Coleridge attended what he considered to be a particularly illustrious dinner party; the company included Walter Scott and Humphry Davy. The host, co-incidentally, was William Sotheby, who in the previous September had been the recipient of Coleridge's letter criticizing Bowles's formal similes. The conversation somehow arrived at the topic of a minor satiric poem, published several years earlier by an anonymous radical; the target of the satire, titled "Fire, Famine, and Slaughter," was Pitt, whom the poem presented as both the ally and, imminently, the victim of the allegorical furies named in the title. Despite his zealous admiration for Pitt, Scott was persuaded to recite the poem, and he performed with evident enthusiasm. But Sotheby was appalled by the violence and malignity of the personal attack on Pitt. At this point Coleridge intervened on behalf of the anonymous poet. He was so taken by the eloquence of his defense that he recorded it years later (probably 1815) in the form of an "Apologetic Preface," and then published it in his *Sibylline Leaves* (1817).[39] For the poem was in fact his.

The interest of Coleridge's "Apologetic Preface"—besides his surprising judgment that it was his "happiest effort in prose composition"—lies in its account of poetic violence. Coleridge's defense depended on the difficult but intriguing claim that poetic agency is inherently incompatible with genuinely violent desire or action. First, Coleridge recalls, he conceded the error of *publishing* so inflammatory a poem. But the concession was, as usual, in the service of a distinction. For Sotheby, the poem's existence was a single, unanalyzable, deplorable fact; but Coleridge deftly insisted on distinguishing the violent act of publication from the creative agency of writing. What insulated the poet from the violence of his own language was first of all his lack of seriousness. The poem was, after all, an extravagant satire, and one might have expected a defense of satiric urbanity and generality, in the mode of Pope or Swift.[40] But the hint of Enlightenment urbanity was merely dropped and abandoned, as Coleridge shifted from the poet's rhetorical stance to his psychological state. The real defense, which the rest of the preface goes on to develop, was the strange theorem that the proliferation of violent images is inversely proportional to the seriousness of violent intentions:

> Could it be supposed, though for a moment, that the author seriously wished what he had thus wildly imagined, even the attempt to palliate an inhumanity so monstrous would be an insult to the hearers. But it seemed to me worthy of consideration, whether the mood of mind and the general state of sensations in which a poet produces such vivid and fantastic images, is likely to co-exist, or is even compatible with, that gloomy and deliberate ferocity which a serious wish to realize them would pre-suppose. It had been often observed . . . that prospects of

pain and evil to others, and in general all deep feelings of revenge, are commonly expressed in a few words, ironically tame,
and mild.

As they unfold this paradox, the next few sentences bring Coleridge's defense into line with the central oppositions we have
traced. Once again the mind is saved from the fanatical violence
of centripetal concentration by the enthusiastic substitutions of
associative fancy. Under the "direful and fiend-like" influence
of revenge, the mind

> seems to take a morbid pleasure in contrasting the intensity of
> its wishes and feelings with the slightness or levity of the expres-
> sions by which they are hinted; and indeed feelings so intense
> and solitary, if they were not precluded (as in almost all cases
> they would be) by a constitutional activity of fancy and associ-
> ation, and by the specific joyousness combined with it, would
> assuredly themselves preclude such activity. Passion, in its own
> quality, is the antagonist of action . . . But the more intense and
> insane the passion is, the fewer and the more fixed are the
> correspondent forms and notions. A rooted hatred, an inveterate
> thirst of revenge, is a sort of madness, and still eddies round its
> favourite object, and exercises as it were a perpetual tautology
> of mind in thoughts and words which admit of no adequate
> substitutes. Like a fish in a globe of glass, it moves restlessly
> round and round the scanty circumference, which it cannot leave
> without losing its vital element.   (*PWC,* II, 1098–1099)

Coleridge goes on to illustrate, first by comparing the style
of death-threats uttered by "two common sailors," then with a
series of literary examples (beginning with exuberant Gratiano
versus implacable Shylock). But the literary examples steadily
gravitate toward the issue of personification. Should we, Coleridge asks,

> hold it either fair or charitable to believe it to have been Dante's
> serious wish that all the persons mentioned by him (many re-
> cently departed, and some even alive at the time,) should actually
> suffer the fantastic and horrible punishments to which he has
> sentenced them in his Hell and Purgatory? Or what shall we say
> of the passages in which Bishop Jeremy Taylor anticipates the
> state of those who, vicious themselves, have been the cause of

vice and misery to their fellow-creatures? Could we endure for a moment to think . . . that a man so natured and so disciplined, did at the time of composing this horrible picture, attach a sober feeling of reality to the phrases? . . . Or do we not rather feel and understand, that these violent words were mere bubbles, flashes and electrical apparitions, from the magic cauldron of a fervid and ebullient fancy, constantly fuelled by an unexampled opulence of language? (*PWC*, II, 1100)

The victims of poetic wrath in Dante and Taylor are not yet reduced to personifications, even though Coleridge's defense requires their dissociation from "a sober feeling of reality." Coleridge in fact denied that "the punishments in the Inferno are strictly allegorical," taking them rather as "*quasi*-allegorical, or conceived in analogy to pure allegory" (*MC*, p. 150). But the appeal to personification becomes explicit when he turns at last to his crucial example, the poetic agency embodied in his own (still unacknowledged) satiric poem:

Were I now to have read by myself for the first time the poem in question, my conclusion, I fully believe, would be, that the writer must have been some man of warm feelings and active fancy; that he had painted to himself the circumstances that accompany war in so many vivid and yet fantastic forms, as proved that neither the images nor the feelings were the result of observation, or in any way derived from realities. I should judge that they were the product of his own seething imagination . . . [and that] he had generalized the causes of the war, and then *personified* the abstract and christened it by the name which he had been accustomed to hear most often associated with its management and measures. I should guess . . . that he had as little notion of a real person of flesh and blood,

Distinguishable in member, joint, or limb,

as Milton had in the grim and terrible phantom (half person, half allegory) which he has placed at the gates of Hell.
(*PWC*, II, 1100–1101; my emphasis)

Under the accusation of violent literalism, allegory becomes the saving medium. Allegorical personification is treated as a token of imaginative power that nevertheless, by its obvious extravagance, guarantees the distinction between imagination and actual belief; it gives access to the power of fanaticism without the attendant dangers of violence and fixation. But the medium is unstable if not illusory; the allusion to Milton's Death reminds us of the personification's obscure and restless oscillation between the fixed materiality of a literal agent and the figurative transparency of a nominal abstraction. In a certain peculiarly overdetermined sense, Milton's Death is the ideal personification, since its unimaginable description—as well as its inconceivable tenor—corresponds to the impossible doubleness of personifications in general.

Such doubleness is also borne out in the argument of the "Apologetic Preface" itself. After completing his fanciful defense of "Fire, Famine, and Slaughter," Coleridge devotes the second half of his essay to an elaborate comparison of Milton and Jeremy Taylor, one of whose sermons had provided the example, cited above, of harmless violence in ecclesiastical rhetoric. What makes the comparison relevant to the first half of the preface is Coleridge's desire to reconcile his profound admiration for both writers, despite their rhetorically violent support of opposing factions in the Civil War. In defending both Milton and Taylor against charges of partisan bigotry, Coleridge follows essentially the line of his apology for his own poem. In his conclusion, however, Coleridge turns to his own contemporaries with an exhortation not to take seriously—as of course they still do—religious controversies that split the nation nearly two hundred years earlier. This time allegory is the culprit, not the savior; instead of insulating the agent from the consequences of imaginative production, allegory is what seduces Coleridge's contemporaries into a personal identification with the past: "It has been too much the fashion first to personify the Church of England, and then to speak of different individuals, who in different ages have been rulers in that church, as if in some strange way they constituted its personal identity. Why should a clergyman of the present day feel interested in the defence of Laud or Sheldon?" (*PWC,* II, 1107). Yet the same process of personification through metonymy—in which an agent associated with the causal operation of an institution or event becomes its personal representative—was exactly the process Coleridge traced in the genesis of his attack on Pitt.

Coleridge was never unwilling to use the same argument more than once. In the same year that he published his "Apologetic Preface" in *Sibylline Leaves,* a bizarre and sadly comical disaster befell his old friend Robert Southey, like Coleridge a former radical whose views had shifted noticeably to the right. As David V. Erdman recounts the incident, Southey "had been urging the suppression of seditious publications. In February [1817] the Radicals piratically published his own republican drama 'on my Uncle Wat Tyler, who knocks out a tax gatherers brains, then rose in rebellion'—as [Southey] merrily described it while writing it in 1794 . . . [Southey's] attorneys sought an injunction from chancery to halt the piracy, but Lord Eldon ruled that there were no property rights in a seditious work" (*EOT,* II, 449–450n4). When Coleridge took up the unpromising cause of rescuing Southey from the multiple ironies of this minor scandal, he adopted not only the same approach but many identical phrases from the "Apologetic Preface." In the second of four articles on Southey's behalf, Coleridge insists, once again, on the need to consider the young writer's probable state of mind. Had he not known the identity of the author of *Wat Tyler,* Coleridge would have guessed him to be "a very young man of warm feelings and active fancy, full of glorious visions concerning the possibilities of human nature"; he would have "seen, that the vivid, yet indistinct images, in which he had painted to himself the evils of war" were the "product of the Poet's own fancy"—and so on, almost verbatim from the defense of "Fire, Famine, and Slaughter" (*EOT,* II, 459).

But in the third article, printed, like the rest, in *The Courier,* Coleridge introduces an astonishing analogy to support his claim that a young poet, "in all his poetic moments, lives in an *ideal* world," and that the poet's characters, "the historic not less than the factitious in *name,* as well as in reality, are mere personifications of general laws" (*EOT,* II, 470–471). His analogous example is Martin Luther, "a case strictly to the point in question." Like Southey, Luther had indulged temporarily in radical sentiments: "Just at the first ferment that afterwards broke out in the horrors of the peasants' war, the heroic Luther, to whose mind, up to that period, no experience was present, no fears, or images of fear, but the wrongs and miseries of the oppressed poor, and the wanton tyranny of the mighty, not only wrote, but published a Circular Letter to the Princes of Germany, which he lived bitterly to regret, and compared with which, indeed, *Wat Tyler* is a mere linctus, a bland emulsion" (*EOT,* II, 471). The tract Coleridge has in mind, as Erdman notes, is Luther's address *To the Christian Nobility of the German Nation* (1520), published when the reformer, however inexperienced, was already in his late thirties. In another context Coleridge describes the work as using "a language so inflammatory," and holding forth "a doctrine which borders so near on the holy right of insurrection, that it may well remain untranslated."[41] But here the document counts as an extravagant poem:

> And for this very reason, that the letter was composed by a Poet (for such Luther eminently was), a Poet fresh from the cloyster and the library, and consequently made up of the common-place generalities of natural feelings and notions peculiarized only by the characteristics of the Poet's own genius, is it equally applicable, and equally inapplicable, to all times and countries ... Now, suppose that the Publishers had printed and sold a translation of this work instead of the *Wat Tyler,* I put the question to Mr. W[illiam] S[mith]'s conscience, whether even he would have considered *Luther* as the criminal to be denounced? I ask, whether, in this instance, he would have referred to the maturer writings of Luther, in which, profiting by his experience, he had so nobly compensated for his former indiscretion by the most eloquent antidotes, as aggravations of the former,—as his motive for holding him up to reprobation,— nay, as convicting him as an Apostate and Renegado?[42]
>
> (*EOT,* II, 471–472)

One can only repeat Erdman's comment: "It is hard to imagine a more damaging case in point" (472n28). Luther recanted his expressions of sympathy for the peasants in a series of tracts published during the spring and summer of 1525, a period extending from the climax of the uprising to the dismal aftermath of its bloody suppression. The first pamphlet, a moderate *Admonition to Peace,* criticized the peasants for their blasphemous millenarianism but otherwise called on both sides to resolve their differences without violence. This work, as Erdman suggests, might fit Coleridge's allusion to the "eloquent antidotes" which Luther applied to his earlier radicalism. What Coleridge fails to mention is the pamphlet that immediately followed when the *Admonition* failed to take effect. The new tract, *Against the Robbing and Murdering Hordes of Peasants,* was a frank invitation to massacre. Its proposals included the famous exhortation to "smite, slay, and stab, secretly or openly, remembering that nothing can be more poisonous, hurtful, or devilish than a rebel."[43] The same doctrine received a more reflective, but hardly less virulent, treatment several months later, when Luther defended his already notorious pamphlet in *An Open Letter on the Harsh Book against the Peasants.* His approach is unchanged: "A rebel is not worth rational arguments, for he does not accept them. You have to answer people like that with a fist, until the sweat drips off their noses. The peasants would not listen . . . so their ears must now be unbuttoned with musket balls till their heads jump off their shoulders." Such violence is warranted because "the rebel has already been tried, judged, condemned, and sentenced to death and everyone is authorized to execute him."[44]

The point of dwelling on this painful episode in Luther's frequently painful career is not to catch Coleridge in a particularly self-defeating case of special pleading, but to suggest the extreme vulnerability of his efforts to insulate poetry from its participation in literal violence. Perhaps the oddest feature of Coleridgean distinctions in general is their almost deliberate implausibility—as if they were designed to collapse under the weight of Coleridge's own examples. But such examples are more than merely self-destructive; as in the case of Milton's personification of death, they often reproduce, in their prior histories or their internal structures, the issues they were meant to resolve. Thus the irony of Coleridge's choosing Luther to prove the nonseriousness of poetic violence runs deeper than the reformer's notorious behavior during the Peasants' War. For Luther's practical politics were at least partly motivated by a theoretical distinction strikingly analogous to the one Coleridge is trying to enforce.

At the center of Luther's pamphlets against the peasants is his powerful doctrine of the "two kingdoms"; Luther posits a radical ethical and political dissociation of temporal authority from the community of believers. While the Christian virtues of mercy and forgiveness, for example, are appropriate to relations among true Christians, the divinely ordained purpose of the state is to maintain a political order embracing true and false Christians alike. Thus the "Scripture passages which speak of mercy apply to the kingdom of God and to Christians, not to the kingdom of the world, for it is a Christian's duty not only to be merciful, but also to endure every kind of suffering." Yet this special moral destiny by no means relieves the individual Christian of obligations even to the most violent expressions of temporal authority: "Those who are in God's kingdom ought to have mercy on everyone . . . and yet not hinder the kingdom of the world in the maintenance of its laws . . .; rather, they should assist it."[45] For Luther, the crucial theological error of the peasants is to collapse the two kingdoms into one by applying the apocalyptic suggestions of Scripture directly to the temporal order. The *Admonition to Peace* already equates millenarianism with the idolatrous appropriation of the Gospel; in the *Open Letter on the Harsh Book* Luther charges that "he who would confuse these two kingdoms—as our false fanatics do— would put wrath into God's kingdom and mercy into the world's kingdom; and that is the same as putting the devil in heaven and God in hell."[46]

The evident irony of Luther's critique lies in the fact that his separation of temporal and theological authority turns into— indeed already is—a version of the literal identification it rejects. In the context of the Peasants' War the rejection of millenarian fanaticism was also an endorsement of temporal authority—an endorsement that for Luther was grounded in an extreme literalization and decontextualization of Scripture, above all of Romans 13 (where Paul had exhorted the then helpless Christian minority not to resist the plainly irresistible Roman Imperium).[47] The peasants' mistake was a literal (practical) application of biblical eschatology to their own political cause; Luther's mistake was to repudiate that error in terms which precisely reproduced it. The consequences of this inconsistency are visible throughout Luther's politics. As Sheldon S. Wolin has remarked, "The problems in Luther's political thought were not the product of a monumental indifference toward politics, but arose from the 'split' nature of a political attitude which oscillated between a disdainful and a frenetic interest in politics and sometimes combined both."[48]

What the analogy between Luther's and Coleridge's distinctions makes clear is the simultaneous necessity and impossibility of separating the "two kingdoms" in each case; whether the nonviolent kingdom is theological or poetic, its independence seems equally precarious. In both cases, an identification of the two realms amounts to idolatry or fanatisicm, to a kind of mad literalization and reduction. But the identification is inevitable, if only because even a refusal of one identity merely establishes another. For Coleridge, moreover, Luther's literalization of Scripture was exactly what made the reformer a "poet" in the first place:

> He deemed himself gifted with supernatural influxes . . . a chosen Warrior . . . against an Army of evil Beings headed by the Prince of the Air. These were no metaphorical beings in his apprehension. He was a Poet indeed, as great a Poet as ever lived in any age or country; but his poetic images were so vivid, that they mastered the Poet's own mind! He was *possessed* with them, as with substances distinct from himself: LUTHER did not *write*, he *acted* Poems. The Bible was a spiritual indeed but not a *figurative* armoury in his belief.[49]

And yet, "When a man mistakes his thoughts for persons and things, he is mad. A madman is properly so defined."[50] Coleridge resolved this contradiction by appealing to still another means of insulating poetry from violence, historical distance. Past imagination is only madness in the demystified present: "The vehement Belief of the Devil and his numberless Army of Rebel Angels was Heroism in Luther—a pitiful anility in Mr. Wilberforce."[51] But Luther's "supernatural influxes" nevertheless take us back to the troublesome topic of enthusiasm and fanaticism in their relation to Coleridge's account of genius. R. A. Knox, the historian of enthusiasm, criticizes George Fox for exactly the mode of literalizing violence that Coleridge imputes to Luther. "The truth is," according to Knox, "that if you adopt the inner light as your rule of faith, it necessarily supersedes and (if need be) overrides the authority of Scripture. Fox could not look upon the Bible as a collection of title-deeds, from which you derive your warrant for this or that; he was living *in* the Bible."[52] It is crucial to note that, in contradiction to recent accounts of the radical force of textuality, the conservative, orthodox, and Catholic views of Scripture insist on its textual status. What makes Luther, for Coleridge, a poet of action is precisely his violation of scriptural textuality. Luther's literalism can be saved from the imputation of fanaticism only by the same protective measures that separate the absolute from the commanding genius. The result, in the article on Southey, is a portrait of childlike eccentricity, of innocence purchased by the loss of power.

Everywhere in Coleridge's pronouncements on poetic agency the process of desynonymization works simultaneously to establish the seriousness of poetry and to save it from the consequences of such seriousness. Poetry itself is a striking case of the Coleridgean medium. Every increase in its power threatens to destroy its special identity, since a fully effective poetry would be indistinguishable from the production of literal belief. Just as enthusiasm must in a sense be quarantined, protected from the social contagion that would degrade it to a mere fanaticism, so poetry must be insulated from the modes of literality it both imitates and inspires.

Allegory and the Self

Coleridge's ambivalence toward personification is symptomatic of a pervasive habit of thought. The fullest account of Coleridgean ambivalence that has yet appeared is Thomas McFarland's extraordinary book on Coleridge's relation to Continental philosophy. According to McFarland, what prevented Coleridge from completing the magnum opus that would have secured his rank in post-Kantian philosophy was his necessarily impossible goal of reconciling the pantheism of Spinoza with the personal freedom of libertarian ethics:

This inability either really to accept or wholeheartedly to reject pantheism is the central truth of Coleridge's philosophical activity. For Coleridge, as for Hamlet . . . this seeming indecision before conflicting claims is a true emblem of his integrity. As with the dilemma of Hamlet, who, not indecisive *in himself,* is confronted with alternatives that *in themselves* admit of no right solution, so . . . Coleridge: he could not resolve the ambivalences of the *Pantheismusstreit* without diminishing one whole side of his awareness and vital commitment.[53]

Confronted by the impressive range of evidence with which McFarland establishes Coleridge's involvement in the pantheism controversy, one is compelled to acknowledge the importance of this particular source of ambivalence. From the point of view of the present study, however, the dilemma over pantheism appears as one more case of Coleridge's oddly abstract desire to establish a medium between identity and difference. To bring the issue into clearer focus, we may consider an instance of the full-blown pantheistic organicism that Coleridge stopped just short of embracing. This example will have the secondary advantage of foregrounding, once again, the role of personification.

In the late 1790s, before taking up his career as an independent systematic philosopher, G. W. F. Hegel composed two remarkable manuscripts (unpublished until 1907) on the historical failure of Christianity—though both texts were, at least in part, veiled attacks on the "Hebraic" moralism of Kant. The second manuscript, *The Spirit of Christianity and Its Fate,* contains an organicist interpretation of Christ's divine sonship with striking affinities to Coleridge's remarks on the consubstantiality of the symbol. Yet Hegel's passage also makes explicit the danger of identification for the independent agency of the self. He begins with the apparently orthodox claim that Jesus' relation to the Father "is a living relation of living beings, a likeness of life." Further, "the son of God is the same essence as the father, and yet for every act of reflective thinking, though only for such thinking, he is a separate essence." The tendency toward total identity is already discernible in the suggestion that separation is purely a figment of intellect. But the full price of identification emerges in the stunning analogy which Hegel now provides:

Even in the expression "A son of the stem of Koresh," for example, which the Arabs use to denote the individual, a single member of the clan, there is the implication that this individual is not simply a part of the whole; the whole does not lie outside him; he himself is just the whole which the entire clan is. This is clear too from the sequel to the manner of waging war peculiar to such a natural, undivided people: every single individual is put to the sword in the most cruel fashion.

And in disappointing contrast to this natural practice on the part of the Arabs, Hegel offers the warfare of liberal modern Europe; for "where each individual does not carry the whole state in himself, but where the bond is only the conceptual one of the same rights for all, war is waged not against the individual, but against the whole which lies outside him. As with any genuinely free people, so among the Arabs, the individual is a part and at the same time the whole. It is true only of objects, of things lifeless, that the whole is other than the parts."[54]

At stake in the difference between Hegel's and Coleridge's accounts of synecdochic identity is the preservation of the empirical human self. To the degree that Coleridge shifts from the nominalist (or, in his own terms, the allegorical) to the realist (literal) notion of synecdoche, he risks the violence of Hegel's Arabs. As Hegel shows, preserving the distinction between the individual and the social totality means retaining a portion of the same enlightened, liberal nominalism that Coleridge struggled to overturn. This political necessity, as much as a resistance to Spinozist theology, accounts for Coleridge's failure to press his organicism to its logical conclusion. Hence his anti-absolutist insistence that the state is not, in fact, an organism, but a medium between a person and a nominal totality or "thing." In an inorganic body, "the whole is nothing more than a collection of the individual parts or phenomena"; whereas in an organic body, for instance "a man," "the whole is the effect of, or results from, the parts; it—the whole—is every thing, and the parts are nothing." But the state is neither kind of body; it is "an intermediate idea between the two—the whole being a result from, and not a mere total of, the parts; and yet not so merging the constituent parts in the result but that the individual exists integrally within it."[55]

The individual's relation to the community is closely tied to the self's relation to truth. For Coleridge, we recall, full "Objectivity" is the identity of "external" fact and subjective truth— but subjective truth is collective, "the Seeing of the millions" that "constitutes to . . . each of the millions the *objectivity* of the sight."[56] Just as the political integrity of the individual depends on a partly nominalist treatment of the group, so the epistemological independence of the self requires a suspension of the force of collective truth. The means of suspension are diverse: fancy, fiction, allegory, and simple error can serve in various contexts to establish the separate identity of the self. Conversely, the subordination of self to truth takes a number of forms. Of these the most dramatic is one that figures prominently in Coleridge's accounts of his own life: conversion.

The importance of traditional models of religious conversion to Coleridge's interpretation of his own life has been highlighted in a recent account by M. H. Abrams. The key text is the passage in the *Biographia* in which Coleridge recounts his inability to accept fully the doctrine of the Incarnation until the completion of a "more thorough revolution in my philosophic principles." He explicitly parallels his own experience to the classic precedent of Augustine. Thus he acknowledges his debt to the "metaphysical notions" of the Unitarians, which "contributed to my final re-conversion to the whole truth in Christ; even as according to his own confession the books of certain Platonic philosophers . . . commenced the rescue of St. Augustine's faith from the same error" (*BL,* I, 205). This passage is not unique; as Abrams notes, "Coleridge repeatedly employs metaphors that posit a triple parallel between religious and moral conversion, political revolution and a radical change in the premisses of philosophy."[57]

Conversion, however, is more than an event of radical change. It functions within a providential scheme of progressive subordination, a movement from the empirical individuality of subjective error to the collective identity of suprapersonal reason or truth. As is clear from the appendix to the *Statesman's Manual* discussed earlier, reason is never the "personal property" of an individual mind (*LS,* p. 70). Later in the same appendix Coleridge identifies the "final cause" of all events as "the increase of Consciousness, in such wise, that whatever part of the terra incognita of our nature the increased consciousness discovers, our will may conquer and bring into subjection to itself under the sovereignty of reason" (*LS*, p. 89). Only a certain obscurity in the relation of the personal will to the suprapersonal reason prevents the subordination of the erring empirical faculties (choice, understanding, fancy, and the like) from becoming their pure eradication, as the individual is eradicated in Hegel's organic community.

For the self, in any collectivist account of truth, is grounded in deviation or error. Thus C. S. Peirce, in the Kantian tradition he shared, though more ambivalently, with Coleridge, wrote: "Ignorance and error are all that distinguish our private selves from the absolute *ego* of pure apperception."[58] According to Peirce, "self-consciousness" itself chiefly expresses the difference between one's own ignorance and the "testimony" of others: "A child hears it said that the stove is hot. But it is not, he says; and, indeed, that central body is not touching it, and only what that touches is hot or cold. But he touches it, and finds the testimony confirmed in a striking way. Thus, he becomes aware of ignorance, and it is necessary to suppose a *self* in which this ignorance can inhere. So testimony gives the first dawning of self-consciousness."[59] The empirical self-consciousness in Peirce's anecdote—a minor episode of conversion—is a glimpse of individual error in a moment of collective truth.

If the empirical self is grounded in error, then the truth about the self—and this may be nothing more mysterious than causal explanation—is always purchased at the cost of individual agency. The explosive power of a conversion experience may derive from a self's earlier resistance to the truth that eventually masters it.[60] The mistake, often made by autobiographers and biographers alike, is to translate this pattern of ideological subordination either into a straightforward process of growth or into a case of illusory wish-fulfillment. Conversion takes place in ironic defiance of individual wishes, which may themselves be products of earlier but ultimately erroneous identifications.

But the irony of self-destruction alone is not enough to account for the fascination that conversion narratives hold even for interpreters who are unsympathetic to the victorious cause.

If conversion subordinates the individual self to some corporate unity of truth, it also reveals that self in the moment of absorbing it. From the perspective of conversion, the self is glimpsed as an alien projection of fantastic error. Such moments of simultaneous self-discovery and self-loss are a psychological analogue to Coleridge's elusive medium between literal and figurative representation. The self they temporarily disclose can easily become the object of nostalgia. But more often than not, I suspect, the exhilaration of conversion derives from the ease with which earlier selves (and selves in this view are always "earlier") are discarded. The scandal that later interpretation may seek to suppress is not the hollowness or wishfulness of conversion, but its almost effortless violence. The Enlightenment goal of transforming self-consciousness into a mode of stable individuation thus depends on granting an imaginary duration to the turn from "error" to "truth."

What makes the Enlightenment project seem feasible is the fact of oscillation, which Coleridge values in such a variety of forms, above all perhaps in the form of "imagination." Conversions, large and small, are endlessly repeatable, as Augustine implicitly acknowledged when he included the "impossibility of sinning" among the gifts to be conferred on the resurrected saints.[61] But the gift of guaranteed perseverance can only be supernatural: "Can any man be sure that he will persevere to the end . . . ? No one can, unless he is assured by some revelation."[62] Milton, in one of those canny revisions of the Augustinian tradition that move him closer to Coleridge, has Raphael describe the uncertainty even of the angels:

> Myself and all th' Angelic Host that stand
> In sight of God enthron'd, our happy state
> Hold, as you yours, while our obedience holds;
> On other surety none; freely we serve,
> Because we freely love, as in our will
> To love or not; in this we stand or fall:
> And some are fallen . . .   (*PL*, V.535–541)

To Milton, even the modicum of independence granted to the angels seems worth an uncertainty that, for Augustine, would amount to a perpetual terror. Yet there is a strange lack of tension in Raphael's account of what should be a condition of terror. The danger of apostasy here already has the reassuring air of artificiality later cultivated by the aesthetics of the sublime. The complacency one detects beneath Raphael's uncertainty is of course borne out by the narrative fact that none of the faithful angels subsequently falls. Raphael is like the model citizen of the liberal commonwealth who persuades himself that his automatic obedience to the law is contingent on a daily choice. When the danger is genuine, as it is in the case of Satan, Eve, and Adam, the complacency gives way to helplessness and fixation. But *Paradise Lost* is filled with moments of imaginative leisure that indulge, like Raphael, in fictional possibilities of apostasy. The modern reader turns to such moments—the epic similes, the pagan allusions, Belial's speech in book II, Eve's account of her first awakening, the invocation to book VII—for images of poetic self-consciousness. While the narrator takes as much pleasure in cancelling such alternatives as he does in presenting them—"thus they relate / Erring"; "But all was false and hollow"; "For thou art Heav'nly, shee an empty dream"—the momentary oscillation between fiction and truth gives an illusion of genuine mediation.

This Enlightenment goal, to secure empirical consciousness in the face of coercive truth, provides perhaps the widest background for the Coleridgean ambivalence toward allegory. For allegory is an extended oscillation between difference and identity, or fiction and truth. In this respect it systematically exemplifies what Coleridge considered the "one great principle . . . common to all the fine arts," "a principle which probably is the condition of all consciousness . . . the perception of identity and contrariety; the least degree of which constitutes likeness, the greatest absolute difference; but the infinite gradations between these two form all the play and all the interest of our intellectual and moral being."[63]

One last notorious episode will return us to the particular example with which this chapter began. At the climax of the *Biographia*, just when he approaches the heart of his crucial chapter *On the imagination, or esemplastic power,* Coleridge in terrupts himself with a fictitious letter from an imaginary friend, who persuades him not to proceed with the publication of a chapter so novel and obscure. The friend found Coleridge's arguments "not only so *new* to me, but so directly the reverse of all I had ever been accustomed to consider as truth," that even if he had understood Coleridge's premises "sufficiently to have admitted them, and had seen the necessity of your conclusions," he would still have "felt as if I had been standing on my head." But the friend goes on to describe the effect of Coleridge's account on his *"feelings,"* and there follows an extraordinary series of oscillating images. Reading Coleridge's chapter was like being placed alone "in one of our largest Gothic cathedrals in a gusty moonlight night of autumn":

> "Now in glimmer, and now in gloom"; often in palpable darkness . . . then suddenly emerging into broad yet visionary lights . . . and ever and anon coming out full upon pictures and stone-work images of great men, with whose *names* I was familiar, but which looked upon me with countenances and an expression, the most dissimilar to all I had been in the habit of connecting with those names. Those whom I had been taught to venerate as almost super-human in magnitude of intellect, I found perched in little fret-work niches, as grotesque dwarfs; while the grotesques, in my hitherto belief, stood guarding the high altar with all the characters of Apotheosis. In short, what I had supposed substances were thinned away into shadows, while every where shadows were deepened into substances:
>
> > "If substance may be call'd what shadow seem'd,
> > For each seem'd either!"   MILTON (*BL,* I, 301)

In what is surely an unparalleled case of overdetermination even for Coleridge, this record of a failed or suspended conversion proclaims a fantastic coincidence of oscillations: the friend, the shadow of Coleridge himself, describes his ambivalence toward the substance of Coleridge's shadowy chapter on imagination with a quotation that exemplifies (by Coleridge's own earlier account) the imagination's power to oscillate between shadow and substance.[64] The issues brought together here through a seemingly incidental allusion to Milton were already linked in a wider context of criticism and poetic practice. Through one of those processes of symbolic particularization that distinguish actual traditions from the ideal generalities of theory, Milton's allegory was already more than a convenient example; it had come to be identified with the troublesome issue of allegorical agency, perceived as a key to poetic power.

Sudden, the sombrous imagery is fled,
Which late my visionary rapture fed:
Thy powerful hand has broke the Gothic chain,
And brought my bosom back to truth again . . .

> Thomas Warton, "Verses on Sir
> Joshua Reynolds's Painted Window
> at New College, Oxford," 1782

2 Milton's Allegory of Sin and Death in Eighteenth-Century Criticism

In part I of his treatise on aesthetics, Edmund Burke sorts human emotions into the two categories, painful and pleasurable, that correspond respectively to our ideas of the sublime and the beautiful. He devotes part II to occasions of the sublime such as terror, obscurity, power, and privation. His first two literary examples, both cited to illustrate sublime obscurity, are from *Paradise Lost*. And the first of these is Milton's description of Death, as that personification appears to Satan at the gates of Hell (II.666–673):

> The other shape,
> If shape it might be call'd that shape had none
> Distinguishable in member, joint, or limb,
> Or substance might be call'd that shadow seem'd,
> For each seem'd either; black it stood as Night,
> Fierce as ten Furies, terrible as Hell,
> And shook a dreadful Dart; what seem'd his head
> The likeness of a Kingly Crown had on.

"In this description," Burke comments, "all is dark, uncertain, confused, terrible, and sublime to the last degree."[1]

However reluctant some of Burke's contemporaries might have been to accept his identification of the sublime with the obscure, they would hardly have questioned his identification of the sublime with Milton. As Samuel H. Monk notes and repeatedly demonstrates, eighteenth-century theoreticians of the sublime continually turned to Milton as "the supreme illustration of whatever particular type of the sublime they advocated."[2] Not only *Paradise Lost* as a whole, but the allegory of Sin and Death in particular, was frequently singled out for its sublimity. Joseph Addison thought the allegory "very strong, and full of Sublime Ideas";[3] his judgment was echoed by a parade of later critics. Francis Atterbury felt his reverence for "the Sublimity of Homer" diminished by a reading of Milton, and he challenged Pope to find anything in the Greek poet "Equal to the Allegory of Sin, and Death, either as to the Greatness, and Justness of the Invention, or the Height and Beauty of the Colouring."[4] In 1744 James Paterson rather perfunctorily labeled the allegory "sublime" and praised it among the other "vastly poetical and inimitable Master-pieces of *Invention, Wit,* and *Elocution*" that abound in book II. Thomas Gibbons, writing after Burke, cited Atterbury's praise of Milton's allegory in support of his own extravagant suggestion that "perhaps there is not a passage in his immortal Work, that of *Paradise Lost,* in which he shines in superior glory."[5]

By choosing the description of Death as an example of the sublime, then, Burke was relying on the incontrovertible authority of a cliché. Yet his praise of Milton's figure, unqualified by any reference to its context in the epic, places Burke on one side of a rather complex debate in eighteenth-century criticism of Milton. From the other side the allegory of Sin and Death was seen as an awkward, if not dangerous, romantic intruder in the essentially realistic space of the epic. A closer look at the fate of the allegory in eighteenth-century criticism generally will take us to the heart of the period's ambivalence over the most extravagant figure it inherited from the Renaissance, the sublime personification.

Like so much else in the eighteenth-century conception of Milton, critical ambivalence over the allegory of Sin and Death begins with Addison's series of essays on *Paradise Lost.*[6] The word "ambivalence," charged as it is with suggestions of unconscious psychological tensions, may in fact be too strong for the doubleness in Addison's judgment of Milton's allegory. Unembarrassed by his mixed feelings, Addison acknowledges them frankly on four separate occasions.[7] In its most general form his attitude can be stated simply: splendid in itself, the allegory does not belong in an epic.[8] Far from rejecting Milton's allegory for any inherent extravagance or obscurity, Addison praises it enthusiastically as "very beautiful and well invented"; "a very finished Piece in its kind, when it is not considered as a Part of an Epic Poem"; and (to repeat a comment cited above) "very strong, and full of Sublime Ideas." Not only is Milton's an excellent allegory, but "[s]uch beautiful, extended Allegories" in general "are certainly some of the finest Compositions of Genius"—though, once again, "not agreeable to the Nature of an Heroic Poem."[9] Addison never objects to "fictitious" agents as such; in his series on the "Pleasures of the Imagination," he devotes one well-known paper to that "kind of Writing, wherein the Poet quite loses sight of Nature, and entertains his Reader's Imagination with the Characters and Actions of such Persons as have many of them no Existence, but what he bestows on them. Such are Fairies, Witches, Magicians, Demons, and departed Spirits. This Mr. *Dryden* calls *the Fairie way of Writing,* which is, indeed, more difficult than any other that depends on the Poet's Fancy, because he has no Pattern to follow in it, and must work altogether out of his own Invention."[10] Prominent among the instances of this kind of writing are personifications, which we encounter "when the Author represents any Passion, Appetite, Virtue or Vice under a visible Shape, and makes it a Person or an Actor in his Poem." And prominent among these Addison mention Milton's Sin and Death—this time without qualification, since their propriety in the epic is not at issue.[11]

Granting Addison's high—and influential—regard for allegorical personifications, we can begin to look more closely at his reasons for excluding them from the highest poetic genre, the epic. One reason is already implicit in his decision to relegate them, however honorifically, to the notably unclassical realm of the "Fairie way of Writing" ("The Ancients have not much of this Poetry among them"). Personified abstractions may seem out of place in the rather Gothic company of "Fairies, Witches, Magicians, Demons, and departed Spirits," the products of medieval "Darkness and Superstition"; aside from Sin and Death and the "whole Creation of the like shadowy Persons in *Spencer*," Addison takes his examples of personification from Ovid and Virgil.[12] Yet classical precedents are outweighed, in the papers on *Paradise Lost,* by Addison's sense that "[s]uch Allegories rather savour of the Spirit of *Spencer* and *Ariosto,* than of *Homer* and *Virgil.*"[13] It is a sense that several of his successors share. In his "Essay on Allegorical Poetry," written with Spenser primarily in mind, John Hughes gives Sin and Death a privileged position as his first example and praises it as "one of the most beautiful Allegories in our Language." Although he also cites several classical examples, Hughes takes pains to emphasize the degree to which his notion of allegory depends on romance. He objects to the application of the term "indifferently to any Poem which contains a cover'd Moral, tho the Story or Fable carries nothing in it that appears visionary or romantick." The kind of allegory that interests Hughes, and that he thinks "may properly challenge the Name," belongs "without the Bounds of Probability or Nature"—just as allegorical agents, he agrees with Addison, belong outside the epic.[14]

The "romantic" provenance of Sin and Death is also taken for granted by Richard Hurd, who attributes the eighteenth-century ambivalence toward "Gothic fictions" to Milton himself. In the urbane nostalgia of Hurd's *Letters on Chivalry and Romance,* Milton's wavering commitment to romance plays a role akin to that his alleged Satanism played according to Blake; Milton is of Arthur's party without quite knowing it:

> Milton, it is true, preferred the classic model to the Gothic. But it was after long hesitation; and his favourite subject was *Arthur and his Knights of the round table.* On this he had fixed for the greater part of his life. What led him to change his mind was, partly, as I suppose, his growing fanaticism; partly,

his ambition to take a different rout from Spenser; but chiefly perhaps, the discredit into which the stories of chivalry had now fallen by the immortal satire of Cervantes. Yet we see thro' all his poetry, where his enthusiasm flames out most, a certain predilection for the legends of chivalry before the fables of Greece.[15]

Toward the end of his discourse, Hurd returns to the question of Milton's Gothic allegiance. Here Sin and Death take on defiant grandeur as survivors, in an increasingly enlightened era, from a sublimely darker age. Before Milton, thanks in part to the revivalist efforts of Spenser,

the new Spirit of Chivalry made a shift to support itself for a time, when reason was but dawning, as we may say, and was just about to gain the ascendant over the portentous spectres of the imagination. It's [*sic*] growing splendour, in the end, put them all to flight, and allowed them no quarter even amongst the poets. So that Milton, as fond as we have seen he was of the Gothic fictions, durst only admit them on the bye . . . Yet, tho' he dropped the tales, he still kept to the allegories of Spenser. And even this liberty was thought too much, as appears from the censure passed on his *Sin* and *Death* by the severer critics.[16]

Despite its inherent attractiveness and imaginative force, then, allegory is to be banished from epic partly because its origins are suspect; it is perceived as an intruder from the foreign world of romance into a decidedly classical genre. For Addison, however, such historical considerations underscore a more crucial incompatibility. As "fictions" in Addison's sense, allegories violate the essentially realistic "texture" of the epic. At stake here is the paramount Aristotelian principle of probability: Addison reluctantly observes "that *Milton* has interwoven in the Texture of his Fable some Particulars which do not seem to have Probability enough for an Epic Poem, particularly in the Actions which he ascribes to *Sin* and *Death,* and the Picture which he draws of the *Lymbo of Vanity,* with other Passages in the second Book."[17] The Probable is not in itself sufficient, Addison later concedes; the Marvellous is also requisite, and he offers a long digression on the necessary balance between the two properties. Ideally, the epic poet ought "to relate such Circumstances, as may produce in the Reader at the same time both Belief and Astonishment." Milton usually strikes such a balance, but the exceptions include the allegory of Sin and Death: "These passages are astonishing, but not credible; the Reader cannot so far impose upon himself as to see a Possibility in them, they are the Description of Dreams and Shadows, not of Things or Persons." Addison does consider the argument, frequently advanced during the Renaissance, that epics after all are always allegorical. Without denying this outright, he insists on the realism at least of the epic surface: "In a Word, besides the hidden Meaning of an Epic Allegory, the plain literal Sense ought to appear probable. The Story should be such as an ordinary Reader may acquiesce in, whatever Natural, Moral, or Political Truth may be discovered in it by Men of greater Penetration."[18]

In these remarks, the criterion of logical probability tends to be replaced by the criterion, rather distinct from it in Aristotle, of ontological possibility. For Aristotle, the former criterion is the decisive one. Commenting on the empirical bias of English neoclassicism in general, and of Hobbes in particular, M. H. Abrams reminds us of Aristotle's paradoxical preference for a probable impossibility over an improbable possibility: "It was Aristotle . . . who made the discussion of possibility and probability a standard element in poetic theory. But to Aristotle, poetic probability had been less an effect of conformity to the external order of things than of the relations of the parts within the work itself; probability, thus conceived, can assimilate even the empirically impossible . . . To Hobbes, truth and likelihood in poetry have become simply a matter of correspondence to the known order of nature."[19] But Addison, for all the empiricism he shares with Hobbes, is not yet disturbed by impossibility as such. His paper on the "Fairie way of Writing" attests to his enthusiasm for "fictitious" beings. Even in the epic he objects not so much to impossible beings as to impossible agents. The second of Addison's papers on *Paradise Lost* is devoted to the poem's "actors," and it is here that his objection to Milton's personifications first appears. For Addison, the status of Sin and Death as "Actors in an Epic Poem" clearly takes precedence over their role as allegorical vehicles. In fact, he is led to his objection by a speculation about the problem of agency that Milton, he supposes, must have encountered. Epics need a variety of agents (compared to the *Iliad,* the *Aeneid* was rather barren in this regard), but the nature of Milton's subject imposed an extraordinary limitation: only two human beings were available. And this, rather than, say, a desire for thematic amplification, drove him to personification: "*Milton* was so sensible of this Defect in the Subject of his Poem, and of the few Characters it would afford him, that he has brought into it two Actors of a Shadowy and Fictitious Nature." The result, a kind of by-product of the need to generate agents, was "a very beautiful and well invented Allegory."[20]

To the twentieth-century reader of *Paradise Lost,* confronted by a baroque profusion of fallen and unfallen angels, by an active and divided deity, by a preternatural energy and variety in the dialogues of Adam and Eve alone—to such a reader, Addison's reasoning is likely to seem odd. Three centuries of poetic "internalization"—the gradual phasing out, after Milton, of agents other than the poet himself—prevent us from sharing such an investment in the direct representation of agency. That investment was itself symptomatic of the early stages of internalization; a theoretical nostalgia for a Homeric richness of character and incident accompanied the increasing dominance in poetic practice of satirical, didactic, and later, more "purely" lyrical forms.[21] However eccentric it may now seem, Addison's sense of Milton's need for additional agents reappears in subsequent writers. Voltaire, in some ways the most extreme eighteenth-century critic of the allegory—the only one I have encountered who objects to its sexual indecency—is almost willing to excuse its inclusion in the epic on grounds directly borrowed from Addison: "I must say, that in general those Fictions, those imaginary Beings, are more agreeable to the Nature of *Milton's* Poem, than to any other; because he hath but two natural Persons for his Actors, I mean *Adam* and *Eve.*" Samuel Johnson, though not in connection with his remarks on Sin and Death, carries Addison's point even further when he notes, as a major "inconvenience" in Milton's design, the fact that "it comprises neither human actions nor human manners."[22]

Despite his appreciation of what he takes to be Milton's plight, Addison concludes that "Persons of such a Chymerical

Existence" as Sin and Death lack "that measure of Probability annexed to them, which is requisite" in epic.[23] In a later paper, devoted specifically to book X, Addison returns to the question of agency. The variety of characters in this book so impresses him that he decides to structure his paper according to the four categories of Milton's "Persons"—"the Celestial, the Infernal, the Human, and the Imaginary." This arrangement places the topic of Sin and Death at the end of the paper, where it provides the occasion for a miniature essay on the problem of epic personification in general, "a Matter which is curious in its kind, and which none of the Criticks have treated of." Having just praised Milton's verbal skill in describing "the Actions" of Sin and Death ("a Reader . . . will be amazed"), and especially the active role of Death as a demonic bridge-builder ("a Work suitable to the Genius of *Milton*"), Addison nevertheless makes it clear that he objects to active, as opposed to merely rhetorical or ornamental, personifications:

> It is certain *Homer* and *Virgil* are full of imaginary Persons, who are very beautiful in Poetry when they are just shown, without being engaged in any Series of Action. *Homer* indeed represents *Sleep* as a Person, and ascribes a short Part to him in his *Iliad;* but we must consider that tho' we now regard such a Person as entirely Shadowy and unsubstantial, the Heathens made Statues of him, placed him in their Temples, and looked upon him as a real Deity. When *Homer* makes use of other such Allegorical Persons it is only in short Expressions, which convey an ordinary Thought to the Mind in the most pleasing manner, and may rather be looked upon as Poetical Phrases than allegorical Descriptions.[24]

Addison gives several instances from the *Iliad* of these "Poetical Phrases," including the catalogue of terrible figures on Athene's aegis (V.738–742). But his own examples to some extent work against him. One personification, Discord (Eris), provides two examples: first as she appears among the figures on the aegis (V.738–742), then as she is called "the Mother of Funerals and Mourning" (Addison's translation) in a later episode (XI.73). Without wanting to pounce too eagerly on his distinction, and remembering that he is no doubt picking examples from memory, we might pause over this instance to notice the willfulness of Addison's decision to read Discord as a metaphor instead of an agent. In the context of the epithet Addison quotes, Eris is explicitly classed among the gods, although she is the only one present to witness this particular clash between the mortal armies (XI.72–75):

> . . . they whirled and fought like
> wolves, and Hate, the Lady of Sorrow, was gladdened to watch
>   them.
> She alone of all the immortals attended this action
> but the other immortals were not there . . .[25]

In an earlier paper, Addison had remembered still another appearance of Eris in the *Iliad;* in that essay he mentioned her as an analogue to an agent no less fully activated than Satan (*PL,* IV.985–989): "*Satan's* cloathing himself with Terror when he prepares for the Combat is truly sublime, and at least equal to *Homer's* Description of Discord celebrated by *Longinus,* or to that of Fame in *Virgil,* who are both represented with their Feet standing upon the Earth, and their Heads reaching above the Clouds."[26] By later ignoring Discord's powerful agency in this episode (IV.439–445)—when she "hurled down bitterness equally between both sides / as she walked through the onslaught making men's pain heavier"—Addison imposes a false stability both on Homer's text and on his own reading.[27] And his association, in this earlier context, of Discord with Satan may indicate why he wants to enforce a distinction between "real" agents and mere emblems or metaphors. Personifications have the unsettling habit of fluctuating between fixed images and active "persons" with the same claim to literal belief as the natural or divine agents who encounter them. In one sense, the energy with which they shift from one mode of representation to another is the measure of their peculiar power. But such mutability, however pronounced in personifications, is a property that may spread, as if by contagion, to other, ostensibly more "literal" agents, as the example of Satan reveals. Not only does Satan, for all his psychological complexity, remain to some extent a theologically precise representation of evil; but, just as the allegorical content of a personification can seem to dissipate, leaving a relatively opaque and independent agent, so Milton frequently allows psychology to lapse as Satan—suitably shrunken, enlarged, or otherwise transformed—freezes into emblematic fixity. The result is sometimes a grotesque surprise, as in Satan's metamorphosis into a serpent (X.509–519). Often, as in the similes of book I or in the passage Addison quotes, the shock of such resolutions of character into image becomes a source of the sublime. Whatever their precise effects in various contexts, such transformations, to paraphrase Addison, savor rather of the spirit of arbitrary magic than of rational Aristotelian mimesis.

Some of the danger implicit in the transformation of rhetorical personifications into agents, then, lies in its apparent reversibility.[28] "Imaginary" agents disrupt the realistic texture of epic partly because they represent an alien mode, but also because they call into question the status of ostensibly "real" or "historical" agents. If personifications are animated through the intensification of metaphor (or more precisely, through the intensification of a metaphoric vehicle at the expense of its supposed "tenor"), then mimetic agents may have a converse tendency to slide "back" into metaphor (that is, the agent may turn out to be the vehicle of a previously unsuspected or forgotten tenor).[29] The reversibility of personifications thus makes the boundary between rhetoric and agency less secure than it might have seemed. As figurative language seems more violent and opaque, agents may seem more transparent and abstract.

Addison does not overtly consider the implications of personification for the surrounding agents in an epic. An explicit objection to the "mixing" of real and imaginary agents does emerge, however, in a later critic clearly writing under Addison's influence: Lord Kames. In his *Elements of Criticism,* Kames at first seems willing to admit "mixt allegorical compositions" in writing, where "the allegory can easily be distinguished from the historical part: no person, for example, mistakes Virgil's Fame for a real being." In painting, as opposed to writing, "such a mixture . . . is intolerable," because real and allegorical characters look too much alike; Kames attacks Rubens in particular for creating a "perpetual jumble."[30] But his apparent acceptance of mixed agents in literary works later disappears in a chapter entitled "Epic and Dramatic Composition," as Kames launches a full-scale assault on epic "machinery." Like Addison, he is willing to accept only the incidental use of personification for rhetorical heightening: "The poetical privilege of animating insensible objects for enlivening a description, is very different from what is termed *machinery,* where deities, angels, devils, or other supernatural powers, are introduced as real personages . . . The former is founded on a natural principle; but can the latter claim the same authority? far from it; nothing is more unnatural."[31]

The "natural principle" to which he alludes here is authentic passion, which provides the authority for a mode of personification superior both to extended allegory and to the merely decorative figures of conventional poetic diction.[32] This new criterion, which moves Kames closer to the Romantics than to Addison, reveals that Kames's objection to supernatural "machinery" in general applies even more forcefully to allegorical agents in particular. Although "an historical poem admits the embellishment of allegory"—indeed, "it amuses the fancy to find abstract terms, by a sort of magic, metamorphos'd into active beings"—nevertheless

allegorical beings should be confined within their own sphere, and never be admitted to mix in the principal action, nor to cooperate in retarding or advancing the catastrophe. This would have a still worse effect than invisible powers; and I am ready to assign the reason. The impression of real existence, essential to an epic poem, is inconsistent with that figurative existence which is essential to an allegory; and therefore no means can more effectively prevent the impression of reality, than to introduce allegorical beings co-operating with those whom we conceive to be really existing . . . An allegorical object, such as Fame in the *Aeneid* . . . may find a place in a description: but to introduce Discord as a real personage, imploring the assistance of Love, as another real personage, to ennervate the courage of the hero, is making these figurative beings act beyond their sphere, and creating a strange jumble of truth and fiction.

Surprisingly, Kames stops short of applying this principle of ontological decorum to the case of Sin and Death. Recognizing that Milton's allegory is "not generally relished," he suggests that "it is not entirely of the same nature with what I have been condemning: in a work comprehending the atchievements [*sic*] of superior beings, there is more room for fancy than where it is confined to human actions."[33] But aside from this demur, Kames makes the basis of Addison's critique abundantly clear: personifications are dangerous not because they are incredible in themselves, but because they undermine the credibility of the agents with which they interact. They spread unreality and should, consequently, be quarantined, "confined within their own sphere." Such confinement can take two forms: the personifications can be excluded from the epic altogether, relegated to properly allegorical works; or they can be restricted to fixed locations within the work, as Virgil's Fame is allowed a "place in a description." Kames's reference to Fame as an acceptably isolated personification in fact echoes Addison's qualified approval of the same figure because "the Part she acts is very short."[34] The desire to quarantine them may explain Addison's preference for personifications that are "just shown." Such a preference, however formalistic its origins, can take on almost ethical force, as when Addison peculiarly attributes the moral sin of hubris—or is it the social sin of presumption?—to the active personifications themselves: "when such Persons are introduced as principal Actors, and engaged in a Series of Adventures, they take too much upon them."[35] (Addison's shift from the passive to the active voice here mimics the unsettling animation he describes.) The danger to be contained is that of imposture. As Kames makes clear, however, the problem is not that readers might mistake the impostor for the genuine agent, but that the spread of imposture will destroy their capacity to believe in anyone.

Addison's and Kames's insistence on the need to restrict the agency of personifications finds powerful endorsement in Johnson's *Life of Milton*.[36] Johnson's utter disparagement of Milton's allegory of Sin and Death is well known; I quote it only to recover the specific issue of agency, often lost in our general sense of Johnson's regard for "realism":

Milton's allegory of Sin and Death is undoubtedly faulty. Sin is indeed the mother of Death, and may be allowed to be the portress of hell; but when they stop the journey of Satan, a journey described as real, and when Death offers him battle, the allegory is broken. That Sin and Death should have shown the way to hell might have been allowed; but they cannot facilitate the passage by building a bridge, because the difficulty of Satan's passage is described as real and sensible, and the bridge ought to be only figurative. The hell assigned to the rebellious spirits is described as not less local than the residence of man. It is placed in some distant part of space, separated from the regions of harmony and order by a chaotic waste and an unoccupied vacuity; but Sin and Death worked up a "mole of aggravated [*sic*] soil," cemented with "asphaltus"; a work too bulky for ideal architects.

This unskillful allegory appears to me one of the greatest faults of the poem; and to this there was no temptation, but the author's opinion of its beauty.[37]

As heavily as he depends on Addison here, to the point of directly borrowing the examples of Victory and Aeschylus' *Prometheus,* Johnson nevertheless departs from his predecessor in one crucial detail. Addison's strictures apply only to the specific case of the "Heroic Poem, which ought to appear credible in its principal Parts."[38] For Johnson, despite his neoclassical affinities, the criterion of genre seems in this instance to have disappeared; it is at most implied by the context. The reappearance of an identical judgment in a different context demonstrates that Johnson rejects elaborate allegorical agency per se: "The employment of allegorical persons always excites conviction of its own absurdity: they may produce effects, but cannot conduct actions; when the phantom is put in motion, it dissolves; thus Discord may raise a mutiny, but Discord cannot conduct a march, nor besiege a town."[39]

The distinction Johnson introduces between static and mobile agency—between producing an effect and conducting an action—raises philosophical questions of the kind he would no doubt have scorned. What is at stake, once again, is the coherence of "real" agency in the contaminating presence of overtly fictional agents. But the desire to confine personifications to static functions may have played a generative as well as a limiting role in poetic practice. In this special case Johnson's views intersect with the general shift from epic and dramatic to lyric forms. If their evident absurdity when in motion deprived personifications of narrative or dramatic roles, the acceptance of their "static agency" rendered them uniquely appropriate to forms in which motion is necessarily curtailed.[40] The eighteenth-century bias against fully active allegorical agents, then, may ironically have contributed to the bewildering proliferation of personifications in mid- and late-century lyrics. Conversely, the Romantic reaction against the conventional repetition of such figures accompanied the partial revival of active allegory in the poetry of Blake and Shelley. For Wordsworth, who avoided both overt allegory and "poetic diction," a naturalized version of static allegorical agency became virtually identical with poetic power (see Chapter 4).

Such speculations, however, take us too quickly beyond the present topic. In this chapter I have isolated three major objections to Milton's Sin and Death: they are too "romantic," too "improbable," and, as shadowy, artificial persons, too active to be admitted to the properly historical genre of the epic. Each of these objections might be justified as an expression of neoclassical concern for decorum (continuity of genre) or for a deeper Aristotelian principle of unity (continuity of action). But, as we have seen, the formal problem of internal consistency shifts into an ontological problem of credibility: the unity of action must be grounded in coherent agents, and coherent agency is threatened by the presence of allegory. Here again one might invoke Aristotle; there is a connection between his insistence on the rational structure of poetic action and his description of character as a consistent pattern of choices, despite his clear subordination of character to plot (*Poetics* 6 and 15). But the neoclassical issues of rationality and consistency are parts of a broader concern, best revealed, perhaps, by an implicit argument in Johnson.

Johnson's rejection of Milton's allegory has a rather surprising relation to what he sees as the poem's essential flaw: its "want of human interest." Sin and Death are dangerous because they threaten the human credibility which the poem already lacks: "The plan of *Paradise Lost* has this inconvenience, that it comprises neither human actions nor human manners. The man and woman who act and suffer are in a state which no other man or woman can ever know. The reader finds no transaction in which he can be engaged, beholds no condition in which he can by any effort of imagination place himself; he has, therefore, little natural curiosity or sympathy."[41] If these remarks are just, they suggest that the trouble with Milton's allegory is not its inconsistency with the poem's essential naturalism, but its special exemplification of a general distance from human concerns. Johnson might reply that, while both the allegory and the poem as a whole indeed lack human interest, they lack it in different ways: the poem is merely inhuman, the allegory inhuman and absurd. More sympathetic critics, such as the ones cited at the beginning of this chapter, would have granted the effect of abstraction and remoteness, but they would have labeled its extreme exemplification in the allegory "sublime." To understand this contemporary alternative to Johnson's strictures, we will need to explore the special relation between the aesthetics of the sublime and the admiration of personifications—despite or perhaps because of the absurdity they risk.

Nor are we only ignorant of the dimensions of the human mind in general, but even of our own. That a Man may be scarce less ignorant of his own powers, than an Oyster of its pearl, or a Rock of its diamond; that he may possess dormant, unsuspected abilities . . . is evident from the sudden eruption of some men, out of perfect obscurity, into publick admiration . . . not more to the world's great surprize, than their own. Few authors of distinction but have experienced something of this nature, at the first beamings of their yet unsuspected Genius on their hitherto dark Composition: The writer starts at it, as at a lucid Meteor in the night; is much surprized; can scarce believe it true. During his happy confusion, it may be said to him, as to *Eve* at the Lake,
What there thou seest, fair creature! is thyself.

> Edward Young, *Conjectures on*
> *Original Composition,* 1759

3 Sublime Personification

In 1947 Bertrand H. Bronson undertook to rescue the eighteenth-century personification from the disrepute into which it had fallen, largely as a result of Romantic and post-Romantic critiques of abstraction. His efforts were seconded by Earl R. Wasserman, who revealed the period's astonishing enthusiasm for personified abstractions by citing an impressive range of eighteenth-century critics, theorists, and apologists. The rehabilitation was completed by Chester F. Chapin, who supplemented a survey of theoretical attitudes toward the figure with a history of its poetic practice.[1] Published by the mid 1950s, these studies have not been superseded; they still provide the indispensable basis of any further research.[2] My aim in the present chapter is not to revise their findings, which are in any case wider in scope than the special topic of sublime personification, but to answer the question raised in the preceding chapter: why did eighteenth-century readers consider (some) personifications sublime, despite their obvious fictionality? The answer lies, I will suggest, in the peculiar ontology of personified abstractions, an ontology that rendered them not only ideal objects of sublime admiration but perfect embodiments of the sublime ideal itself. This answer will only make sense, however, after an account of the self-reflexive logic of the sublime experience, as analyzed by its most impressive theorists, Burke and Kant.

Artificial Terror

The most notorious obstacle confronting historians of the sublime is the difficulty of deciding who or what, in any given case, the critic means to call "sublime": the object itself (for example, a natural prospect or a poem), the agent who produces it (God or the poet), or the agent who encounters it (the spectator or reader).[3] In eighteenth-century accounts of the sublime in literature, a poetic figure can become sublime either when it reveals the genius of the poet or when it occasions a sublime experience in the reader. Both sources of sublimity—the poet's invention and the reader's experience—are invoked in eighteenth-century comments on sublime personification. Wasserman, supporting his assertion that personification "was usually associated with the esthetics of the sublime," quotes Mrs. Barbauld on the power of personification in Collins: "In his endeavors to embody the fleeting forms of mind, and clothe them with correspondent imagery, he is not unfrequently obscure; but even when obscure, the reader who possesses congenial feelings is not ill pleased to find his faculties put upon the stretch in the search of those sublime ideas which are apt, from their shadowy nature, to elude the grasp of the mind."[4] Mrs. Barbauld is chiefly interested in personifications as evidence of Collins' inventive genius, but her focus shifts easily to the pleasure readers take in the exercise of their own imaginative agency. Conversely, Burke introduces Milton's figure of Death for the sake of its impact on the astonished reader, but at the same time records his admiration of Milton's genius. Burke identifies Milton's inventive power as itself an instance of the sublime: "His description of Death in the second book is admirably studied; it is astonishing with what a gloomy pomp, with what a significant and expressive uncertainty of strokes and colouring he has finished the portrait of the kind of terrors" (*PE,* p. 59). Yet Burke has earlier reminded us that "astonishment . . . is the effect of the sublime in its highest degree" (*PE,* p. 57). We are thus left uncertain whether the real source of sublimity here is the obscurity of Milton's description or the mystery of Milton's own agency.[5]

These alternative sources of the sublime are already established by Longinus, who also provides the rudiments for interpreting their connection. In the Longinian account, they overlap in two different ways. In his first chapter (1.4), Longinus divides the sublime moment into two interdependent effects: first, a stroke of rhetoric that overpowers the audience; and second, a revelation of genius in the speaker's capacity to exceed the normal constraints of argument: "For the *Sublime* not only persuades, but even throws an audience into transport . . . Dexterity of invention, and good order and oeconomy in composition, are not to be discerned in one or two passages, nor scarcely sometimes from the whole texture of a discourse; but the *Sublime,* when seasonably addressed, with the rapid force of lightning has borne down all before it, and shown at one stroke the compacted might of genius."[6] At this point in the treatise Longinus has yet to explain why the orator's sudden triumph should transport rather than humiliate the audience. But later on (7.2), in a second description of the relation between the speaker's power and the audience's experience, he introduces (without elaborating it) the crucial principle of *identification:* "For the mind is naturally elevated by the true *Sublime,* and so sensibly affected with its lively strokes, that it swells in transport and an inward pride, as if what was only heard had been the product of its own invention."[7]

The rhetorician's essentially practical interest led him no further into the psychology of such identifications than these and a few similar remarks suggest. For the eighteenth-century theorists, however, the mind's ability to appropriate an external power became a central concern. If the precise mechanism of identification is merely left opaque by Longinus, who seems to imagine a straightforward transfer of power from one source to another, it becomes genuinely puzzling when the power is no longer simply grand, but threatening. The novel element in eighteenth-century accounts, epitomized by Burke and ratified, in this respect, by Kant, is an overt emphasis on experiences seemingly opposed to the "inward pride" of the self—occasions of danger, uncertainty, and above all, terror.[8] "Indeed," Burke asserts in a passage added for emphasis to his second edition (1759), "terror is in all cases whatsoever, either more openly or latently the ruling principle of the sublime" (*PE*, p. 58).[9] To Edward Gibbon, Burke's insistence on terror seems to work against the Longinian notion of proud identification: "It is surprizing how much Longinus and Mr. Bourke differ as to their idea of the operations of the sublime in our minds. The one considers it as exalting us with a conscious pride and courage, and the other as astonishing every faculty, and depressing the soul itself with terror and amazement."[10] But Thomas Green, commenting on Gibbon, recovers a crucial qualification: Burke "makes the sublime turn, indeed, on pain and danger, which, *when near*, overpower and oppress; but on pain and danger *removed;* in which case, the mind, arrogating to itself some portion of the importance which these qualities confer, feels that swelling and triumph, that glorying and sense of inward greatness, which he expressly quotes Longinus as ascribing to the Sublime."[11]

Green is thinking of Burke's striking discussion of ambition, a discussion that concludes with the only direct reference to Longinus in the body of the *Enquiry*.[12] The passage happens also to be the moment in which Burke stands closest to the mainstream of eighteenth-century criticism—and closest to Kant:

Ambition

Although imitation is one of the great instruments used by providence in bringing our nature towards its perfection, yet if men gave themselves up to imitation entirely, and each followed the other, and so on in an eternal circle, it is easy to see that there never could be any improvement amongst them. Men must remain as brutes do, the same at the end that they are at this day, and that they were in the beginning of the world. To prevent this, God has planted in man a sense of ambition, and a satisfaction arising from the contemplation of his excelling his fellows in something deemed valuable amongst them. It is this passion that drives men to all the ways we see in use of signalizing themselves, and that tends to make whatever excites in a man the idea of this distinction so very pleasant. It has been so strong as to make very miserable men take comfort that they were supreme in misery; and certain it is, that where we cannot distinguish ourselves by something excellent, we begin to take a complacency in some singular infirmities, follies, or defects of one kind or other. It is on this principle that flattery is so prevalent; for flattery is no more than what raises in a man's mind an idea of a preference which he has not. Now whatever either on good or upon bad grounds tends to raise a man in his own opinion, produces a sort of swelling and triumph that is extremely grateful to the human mind; and this swelling is never more perceived, nor operates with more force, than when without danger we are conversant with terrible objects, the mind always claiming to itself some part of the dignity and importance of the things which it contemplates. Hence proceeds what Longinus has observed of that glorying and sense of inward greatness, that always fills the reader of such passages in poets and orators as are sublime; it is what every man must have felt in himself upon such occasions.   (*PE*, pp. 50–51)

Among the several puzzling features of this passage is its uneasy relation to Burke's larger argument. At the same moment that Burke locates himself most explicitly within the tradition of sublime aesthetics, he seems furthest away from the principles argued so insistently elsewhere in his treatise. Throughout part I, Burke has been calling for a sharp distinction between passions that turn on pain and on pleasure; the sublime derives not from any "positive pleasure," but from a species of modified pain that Burke calls "delight." The sublime thus takes its place among the passions belonging to "self-preservation," rather than among the pleasurable emotions Burke identifies with "society" (*PE*, pp. 35–40). The difficulty arises when we remember that ambition, treated here as a source of the sublime, is expressly classed among the social, not the self-preservative, passions. It will take a moment to sort out what has gone wrong.

Burke has earlier divided society into two categories: "The

society of the *sexes,* which answers the purposes of propagation; and next, that more *general society,* which we have with men and with other animals, and . . . even with the inanimate world." Only the first of these does Burke associate exclusively with pleasure. The second includes passions "of a complicated kind"; they "branch out into a variety of forms agreeable to that variety of ends they are to serve in the great chain of society. The three principal links in this chain are *sympathy, imitation,* and *ambition*" *(PE,* pp. 40, 44). Among these, only imitation is treated as a source of unmixed pleasure; Burke's account of it admittedly follows Aristotle's *Poetics* 4 *(PE,* pp. 49–50). Sympathy, "a sort of substitution, by which we are put into the place of another man," can involve either pleasure or pain; in the latter case it becomes a source of the sublime, as in our enjoyment of tragedy. Even a real calamity (provided we are not among the victims) "always touches with delight," though our identification with the victims' suffering "prompts us to relieve ourselves in relieving those who suffer" *(PE,* pp. 44–48).

Sympathy, then, provides a point of contact between the opposing passions of society and of self-preservation; it subordinates the individuating experience of the sublime to social needs. Ambition enters Burke's argument, rather surprisingly, as a second source of reconciliation, another providential guarantee. What drops out of the discussion of ambition, however, is any mention of self-preservation. In the case of sympathy, the sublime "delight" is still directly linked to an experience of danger or pain, only diminished by the fact that we are not the actual sufferers. But the mechanism of ambition is harder to explain in Burke's terms. The drive for supremacy—the Satanic capacity to "take comfort" in the fact that one is at least "supreme in misery"—scarcely lends itself to a simple notion of self-preservation. The "swelling and triumph" produced when a man rises "in his own opinion" seem painless enough. Burke's reference to the "terrible objects" that raise such "swelling" to a sublime intensity certainly connects this passage to his general account of terror as the chief occasion of self-preservative excitement. But here these objects contribute "dignity and importance" rather than fear. Moreover Burke sees the mind as actively "claiming" rather than passively submitting to the power it encounters. What should have operated as an external threat—its force diminished only by the accidental condition that we are not really in danger—is somehow converted into the self's own power, or rather referred to a power in the self, since Burke makes no claim for the authenticity of such appropriation: a man's self-esteem can after all be raised "either on good or upon bad grounds."

But what especially sets the passage apart from the rest of Burke's argument is the role played here by reflection. Although Burke clearly thinks of ambition itself as an instinct, implanted by God, its activation by the sublime experience requires precisely the sort of intellectual operation that Burke elsewhere denies. Self-satisfaction depends on the "contemplation" of one's own excellence; the mind claims a portion of the power it "contemplates." Even flattery "raises in a man's mind an *idea* of a preference which he has not." Such intellectualism is obviously opposed to the mode of physiological explanation Burke offers later on (part IV) when he traces the "efficient cause" of delight to the exercise of our finer organs. And he explicitly rejects the kind of reasoning implicit in this passage during his earlier discussion of sympathy:

> It is a common observation, that objects which in the reality would shock, are in tragical, and such like representations, the source of a very high species of pleasure. This taken as a fact, has been the cause of much reasoning. The satisfaction has been commonly attributed, first, to the comfort we receive in *considering* that so melancholy a story is no more than a fiction; and next, to the *contemplation* of our own freedom from the evils which we see represented. I am afraid it is a practice much too common in inquiries of this nature, to attribute the cause of feelings which merely arise from the mechanical structure of our bodies, or from the natural frame and constitution of our minds, to certain conclusions of the reasoning faculty on the objects presented to us; for I should imagine, that the influence of reason in producing our passions is nothing near so extensive as it is commonly believed. (*PE,* pp. 44–45; emphasis added)

The key terms here are "considering" and, once again, "contemplation"; they point to the interference of intellect in a process whose unreflective immediacy Burke above all wants to establish. By placing this more typical passage next to the discussion of ambition, we arrive at two competing accounts of the sublime. At stake in the choice between them is not simply Burke's cherished physiology, but the seriousness of the sublime as an authentic experience rather than an act of self-congratulation. In both passages Burke is characteristically urbane; in the discussion of literary sympathy he deftly attacks the pretensions of traditional rationalist criticism. But the irony of the section on ambition reaches further. Reason is still finally subject to the operations of instinct, which are in turn subordinated to a larger providential scheme. But the sublime itself now depends on an act of reference: the terrible object must be taken to signify a power in the self. The sublime experience, no longer an instinctive reflex, turns out to be doubly inauthentic: first, because the power thus internalized is no real property of the self; second, because even this illusory aggrandizement is in the service not of the self but of providence, which conforms even the vice of pride to social ends. Burke's account of ambition thus verges on both satire and allegory. The influence of satire is visible in his reference to the vanity of cherishing even one's "singular infirmities, follies, or defects" for the negative distinction they confer. And we may detect the pressure of allegory in Burke's confident attribution of all such individuating tendencies to the providential order. In any case the moment of sublime self-inflation comes perilously close to ironic deflation as its essentially figurative structure is revealed.

Credit for the full elaboration of that structure belongs to Kant. The appearance of Kant's "Analytik des Erhabenen" in a study of British poetics needs a word of explanation, despite, or perhaps because of, the precedent established by Samuel H. Monk. Monk's important history of the sublime has become suspect for its treatment of Kant's aesthetic "subjectivism" as the "unconscious goal" of the less rigorous English theories.[13] The issue of subjectivism is a slippery one; even Burke, for all his willingness to identify and sort out "terrible objects," always takes such objects to be the sources or occasions of the sublime experience, not its immediate "efficient cause," which he refers instead to the interaction of bodily and mental events (*PE*, pp.

129–130). And the subjective character of experience was after all a commonplace assumption of the empiricism and associationism that inform virtually every English account. But Kant was nevertheless the first to explore the logic of the crucial reflective turn—the moment of identification—whose figurative structure was already implicit in Longinus and his English successors.

Self-Consciousness in the Kantian Sublime

For Kant, the sublime experience always involves a temporary failure or humiliation of the subject. The occasions of such failure take two major forms. In the "mathematical sublime," an encounter with extreme magnitude, for example a limitless numerical series or a vast phenomenon of nature, challenges the imagination to an impossible effort of comprehension. In the "dynamical sublime," the source of challenge is the violent power of nature (exemplified by storms, waterfalls, threatening rocks), which we recognize the futility of resisting. In both cases, however, the humiliation is short-lived, since failure on the level of sense is interpreted as a sign of the mind's supersensible vocation. The agent responsible for this providential translation of defeat into victory is the reason, which takes the moment of discontinuity as an opportunity to assert its own superior claims. Reason displays itself in the mind's capacity to think a totality that it cannot sensuously represent, and to think a superiority to nature that it cannot naturally achieve: *"The sublime is that, the mere capacity of thinking which evidences a faculty of mind transcending every standard of sense."* Since the real source of sublimity is precisely this faculty, objects outside the mind are sublime only in a secondary or figurative sense, through our "substitution of a respect (*Achtung*) for the Object in place of one for the idea of humanity in our own self—the Subject."[14]

Both types of the Kantian sublime have equivalents in Burke, but the dynamical sublime is more immediately connected to Burke's dominant emphasis on terror; it also raises the issue of figurality in a more explicit way. For Kant as for Burke, "the aesthetic judgment can only deem nature a might (*Macht*), and so dynamically sublime, in so far as it is looked upon as an object of fear." Yet genuine or immediate fear is ruled out by its hostility to disinterested judgment: "One who is in a state of fear" can no more judge the sublime "than one captivated by inclination and appetite" can judge the beautiful. Hence Kant relies on the Burkean proviso that our own position be secure. And this requirement of personal security gives at least the first stage of the experience an overtly imaginary character. Although genuine fear is excluded, "we may look upon an object as *fearful*, and yet not be afraid *of* it, that is, our estimate takes the form of our simply *picturing to ourselves* the case of our wishing to offer some resistance to it, and recognizing that all such resistance would be quite futile." This combination of putative danger and actual safety gives reason its opportunity. Just as, in the mathematical sublime, the limitation of our imaging power reveals "in our rational faculty" a "non-sensuous standard," so here

> in just the same way the irresistibility of the might of nature forces upon us the recognition of our physical helplessness as beings of nature, but at the same time reveals a faculty of estimating ourselves as independent of nature, and discovers a preeminence above nature that is the foundation of a self-preservation of quite another kind . . . This saves humanity in our own person from humiliation, even though as mortal men we have to submit to external violence (*Gewalt*). In this way external nature is not estimated in our aesthetic judgment as sublime so far as exciting fear, but rather because it challenges our power (one not of nature) to regard as small those things of which we are wont to be solicitous (worldly goods, health, and life), and hence to regard its might (to which in these matters we are no doubt subject) as exercising over us and our personality no such rude dominion (*Gewalt*) that we should bow down before it, once the question becomes one of our highest principles and of our asserting or forsaking them.[15]

The last turn in this argument, the conversion of external danger into a moral imperative rather than merely a psychological pleasure as in Burke, is the crucial one for Kant. Yet as Kant fully recognizes, the imaginary status of the original crisis raises questions about the seriousness of its ethical resolution. The crisis is, after all, self-induced; nature is merely its occasion: "Therefore nature is here called sublime merely because it raises the imagination to a presentation of those cases in which the mind can make itself sensible (*sich fühlbar machen kann*) of the appropriate sublimity of the sphere of its own being (*die einege Erhabenheit seiner Bestimmung*), even above nature." And Kant meets the implication of this observation head-on: "This estimation of ourselves loses nothing by the fact that we must see ourselves safe in order to feel this soul-stirring delight—a fact from which it might be plausibly argued (*es scheinen möchte*) that, as there is no seriousness (*Ernst*) in the danger, so there is just as little seriousness in the sublimity of our faculty of soul."[16]

Precisely this plausible argument has been advanced in a fascinating recent commentary by Thomas Weiskel. Weiskel's account of "Kant's fictional moment" concentrates on the mathematical sublime, in which, he suggests, the reason engineers the imagination's failure "in order to discover itself freshly in an attitude of awe." The sublime thus expresses reason's deliberate strategy of sacrifice and subordination in the service of its own ambition: "The cause of the sublime is the *aggrandizement of reason at the expense of reality and the imaginative apprehension of reality*."[17] For Weiskel, this interior power struggle among personified faculties of the mind has all the markings of psychic conflict as represented in classical psychoanalysis.[18] In the mathematical sublime the domination of a lower by a higher faculty suggests the mechanism of repression. In the dynamical sublime, where the higher faculty (reason or, for Weiskel and Freud, the superego) strengthens itself through reference to an external threat, the relevant mechanism is identification or introjection, which neutralizes oedipal anxiety by internalizng the terrifying image of the father.[19] Despite his occasional use of alternative emphases in the psychoanalytic tradition—emphases, for example, on narcissism or pre-oedipal (oral) anxiety—Weiskel's chief model is the oedipus complex. In a critical extension of Weiskel's argument Neil Hertz suggests that Weiskel's preference for oedipal structures itself partakes of the fictional sort of strategy Weiskel exposes in Kant. The prominence of the oedipal complex, with its geometric symmetries of conflict and identification, reflects the "scholar's *wish*" to resolve the chaotic plurality of experience—pre-oedipal or literary—into manageable and reassuring totalities.[20] But Hertz shares Weiskel's assumption that the goal of Kant's sublime is self-aggrandizement, despite a superficial appearance of crisis. The crisis itself, "even before its recuperation as sublime exaltation," is "a confirmation of the unitary status of the self. A passage to the limit may seem lurid, but it has its ethical and metaphysical uses."[21]

These arguments, only crudely summarized here, lend subtlety and precision to the ironic reading Kant attempted to preclude. Yet Kant's proleptic answer to that reading may suggest that the emphasis on self-confirmation is misplaced. According to Hertz, the point of the sublime is to arrange "a one-to-one confrontation" between the self and some external but unified "blocking" agent, all for the sake of "that supererogatory identification with the blocking agent that is the guarantor of the self's own integrity as an agent."[22] But which self, and what kind of integrity? Kant, in the sentence immediately following his acknowledgment of the sublime's apparent lack of seriousness, deftly splits the self in two. Just as the occasion of the sublime experience is divided between an imaginary danger and an actual condition of safety, so the subject of the experience divides into an empirical self and a supersensible locus of value or truth, with which the empirical self is only ironically or intermittently identified: "For here the delight only concerns the *province (Bestimmung)* of our faculty disclosed in such a case, so far as this faculty has its root in our nature; notwithstanding that its development and exercise is left to ourselves and remains an obligation. Here indeed there is truth—no matter how conscious a man, when he stretches his reflection so far abroad, may be of his actual present helplessness."[23]

Kant's point here is not that the empirical agent is permanently excluded from identification with the exalted *Bestimmung*—the destiny, vocation, law, or *telos*—of collective human nature; without at least a temporary identification the empirical delight of the experience would be incomprehensible. But the seriousness of the sublime depends precisely on denying the necessity of that identity. Overidentification—the assumption that the self is genuinely in the state of truth—would cancel the essential negativity of the presentation of reason and collapse the sublime into the satirical caricature of self-congratulation depicted in Burke's section on ambition. There is irony in Kant's account, but not against the agency of reason. Like God, reason has no need of the empirical individual, whose individuality is a measure of deviation from reason. Some degree of conformity to reason is a prerequisite for the sublime, since without it the perception of one's inadequacy would replace admiration with geniune humiliation and fear. Kant himself addresses the topic of God's wrath. One who is "actually in a state of fear, finding in himself good reason to be so, because he is conscious of offending . . . is far from being in the frame of mind for admiring the divine greatness." Instead, one needs a consciousness "of having a disposition that is upright and acceptable to God" in order to admire an omnipotent wrath no longer directed against oneself. The agent's integrity, such as it is, thus *precedes* the sublime experience, which reimposes the divine claim as a further obligation to conform, and also reestablishes the fact of the agent's deviation. Hence even religious humility—"an uncompromising judgment" on one's "shortcomings"—is "a sublime temper of the mind voluntarily to undergo the pain of remorse as a means of more and more effectually eradicating its cause."[24]

Because the empirical self is only contingently related to the unitary standard of reason, Kant is unembarrassed by the dependence of the sublime on education. We automatically assume that others will agree with our judgments on beauty, which for Kant entails the harmony of empirical faculties, imagination and understanding. But we cannot be so confident in the case of the sublime:

> In fact, without the development of moral ideas, that which, thanks to preparatory culture, we call sublime, merely strikes the untutored man as terrifying . . . So the simple-minded, and, for the most part, intelligent, Savoyard peasant, (as Herr von Saussure relates,) unhesitatingly called all lovers of snow-mountains fools . . .

But the fact that culture is requisite for the judgment upon the sublime in nature (more than for that upon the beautiful) does not involve its being an originial product of culture and something introduced in a more or less conventional way into society. Rather is it in human nature that its foundations are laid, and, in fact, in that which, at once with common understanding, we may expect every one to possess and may require of him, namely, a native capacity for the feeling for (practical) ideas, i.e. for moral feeling.[25]

Once again the scandal of mystification is directly confronted, and once again Kant's answer is to give up empirical authenticity without a struggle. The moral *Bestimmung* remains in force as a true predicate of universal human nature despite the sheer contingency of anyone's having or lacking the empirical equipment to realize it. In the face of this logical and metaphysical split in Kant's conception of agency—a dualism of course reflected in Kant's ethical philosophy generally—a psychological interest in repression or self-confirmation is likely to seem irrelevant.[26]

Yet Hertz is right. The goal of the sublime *is* a certain stabilization of the self, though not quite by means of a unifying identification. The self whose stability is served by the sublime is a self produced in the moment of the sublime. It signifies a partial or temporary coincidence of reason and the empirical agent. This structure of partial identification—which depends as much on difference as it does on identity—is the one we have already encountered in the Coleridgean ambivalence toward poetic power. The danger of utter difference or sheer fictionality is easily handled; rather than threatening the sublime experience, this condition prevents it from ever beginning. The agent who recognizes no sublimity of disposition in himself is simply condemned to humiliating fear or indifference. The opposing danger of total identificaton, the collapse of all difference between reason and empirical consciousness, is figured, for Kant as for Coleridge, in the issue of fanaticism. And here the prescriptive negativity of Kant's sublime comes into play: "This pure, elevating, merely negative presentation of morality involves . . . no fear of *fanaticism* (*Schwärmerei*), which is a *delusion* that would *will some* VISION *beyond all the bounds of sensibility;* i.e. would dream according to principles (rational raving [*mit Vernunft rasen*]). The safeguard is the purely negative character of the presentation. For *the inscrutability of the idea of freedom* precludes all positive presentation."²⁷

According to Weiskel, this passage confirms the operation of repression in Kant's scheme; the imagination is "limited to a passive representing of the sensible" in order to preserve the self-aggrandizing autonomy of reason.²⁸ What fanaticism threatens, however, is not so much the truth of reason as the distance between that truth and the empirical self. Even without fanaticism, the imagination is far from passive. Kant, like Coleridge, distinguishes fanaticism from a more benevolent mode of imaginative power, enthusiasm. Unlike fanaticism, enthusiasm is at least compatible with the sublime. The distinction lies in the fact that, in enthusiasm, the negative character of reason's presentation is preserved. In the paragraph immediately preceding the account of fanaticism, Kant explains why difference by no means translates into passivity. Kant's example is the exhilaration of Hebraic iconoclasm:

> We have no reason to fear that the feeling of the sublime will suffer from an abstract mode of presentation . . . For though the imagination, no doubt, finds nothing beyond the sensible world to which it can lay hold, still this thrusting aside of the sensible barriers gives it a feeling of being unbounded . . . Perhaps there is no more sublime passage in the Jewish Law than the commandment: Thou shalt not make unto thee any graven image, or any likeness of any thing that is in heaven or on earth, or under the earth, &c. This commandment can alone explain the enthusiasm which the Jewish people, in their moral period, felt for their religion when comparing themselves with others.

And the example oddly carries him from an insistence on abstraction to an almost Miltonic or Blakean protest against exactly the sort of repression charged by Weiskel. For Kant, it is the presence, not the absence, of images that serves repression:

> For when nothing any longer meets the eye of sense, and the unmistakable and ineffaceable idea of morality is left in possession of the field, there would be need rather of tempering the

ardour of an unbounded imagination to prevent it rising to enthusiasm, than of seeking to lend these ideas the aid of images
and childish devices for fear of their being wanting in potency.
For this reason governments have gladly let religion be fully
equipped with these accessories, seeking in this way to relieve
their subjects of the exertion, but to deprive them, at the same
time, of the ability, required for expanding their spiritual powers
beyond the limits arbitrarily laid down for them, and which
facilitate their being treated as though they were merely passive.[29]

The imagination is both preserved and inflamed by the inaccessibility of its supersensible object. What then, if not the
threat of imaginative excess, is the danger of fanaticism? Kant's
answer takes us back both to the world of Enlightenment satire,
implicit in Burke's account of ambition, and to the Coleridgean
portrait of brooding malice: "If enthusiasm is comparable to
delirium (*Wahnsinn*), fanaticism may be compared to *mania*
(*Wahnwitz*). Of these the latter is least of all compatible with
the sublime, for it is *profoundly* ridiculous. In enthusiasm, as an
affection, the imagination is unbridled; in fanaticism, as a deep-
seated, brooding passion, it is anomalous. The first is a transitory
accident to which the healthiest understanding is liable to become at times the victim; the second is an undermining disease."[30]

In the brooding, obsessive fixity of Kant's fanatic—a fixity
achieved through a visionary identification of empirical consciousness with the idea of reason—one recognizes the frozen
agency of the personification. To imagine such a figure, the
personification of an ideal incapable of literal embodiment, is
to enter a version of the dynamical sublime by subjecting oneself
to an imaginary danger of fixation. Although genuine fanaticism
in the subject is inimical to the sublime experience, the fanatic
himself virtually personifies the sublime occasion. The fanatic's
identification with reason is a delusion that falsely collapses the
distance between empirical agency and universal obligation, just
as a momentary pretense of danger collapses the agent's safe
distance from some threatening object. The fanatic, mindlessly
absorbed by delusion, is not himself sublime or aware of sub-

limity; to appreciate the paradox of fanaticism one must *not* be a fanatic. Fanaticism stands both for the aim and the destruction of sublime identification; the moment of identity is also a lapse into bathos. The Kantian subject is thus condemned, as a kind of negative fanatic, to oscillate between sympathy and irony in relation to the self's identification with truth.[31]

Implications for Poetic Practice

Kant's ambivalence toward the idealization of self parallels the Enlightened ambivalence toward allegory, discussed in the first two chapters of this book. Both Kant and the English critics admire the imagination's power to identify empirical consciousness with abstract ideality. But in both cases such admiration is thwarted by fear of the consequences for the empirical individual. Yet "fear" is too stong, too psychologically precise a term for what is at least partly an artificial danger. After his awakening, by Hume, from the "dogmatic slumber" of rationalism, Kant was in little danger of backsliding; his commitment to important elements of empiricism remained secure throughout his development of the critical philosophy.[32] Kant's vision of fanaticism is itself an impossible satirical ideal, a product of the fictional logic of the sublime, as the excessive language of pathology ("an undermining disease") and of oxymoron ("rational raving") suggests. Similarly, in eighteenth-century responses to Renaissance allegory, from Addison onward, hints of genuine admiration or uneasiness are often matched by antiquarian complacency and condescension. This is only to say that the interest in fanaticism, as in archaic modes of thought, is as much literary and ideological as it is psychological. The point of fanaticism is to establish, by means of contrast, the Enlightenment's sense of itself. The fanatic, like the allegorical personification, expresses an Enlightened fantasy of pre-Enlightened agency. (How far such fantasies also anticipated or responded to what would emerge as real threats to Enlightened notions of agency—threats from Rousseau, Fichte, Wordsworth, evangelicalism, and events in France—would be hard to measure in general terms.)

This paradoxical desire for safe participation in ideal or fixated modes of agency accounts for the special relation of personification to the sublime. Personification in general no doubt served the range of stylistic functions surveyed by Bronson, Wasserman, and Chapin. But sublime personifications uniquely balance the conflicting criteria of power and distance required by the Enlightened stance of urbane admiration. With its individuality utterly absorbed by the ideal it embodies, the personification is the perfect fanatic. It is both devoid of empirical consiousness and perfectly, formally conscious of itself. But the reassuring condition of such perfection is its sheer and obvious fictionality.

Perfect self-consciousness accounts for one of the strangest features of many personifications, their oddly stylized reflexiveness. This is the peculiarity Coleridge criticized, for example, in Spenser. In marginalia on Robert Anderson's *Poets of Great Britain* (1793–1807), Coleridge singles out the description of dissemblance during the masque of Cupid in Busyrane's castle (*Faerie Queene,* III.xii.14). The trouble with this figure—whose "bright browes were deckt with *borrowed* hair"—is that it confuses description with allegorical content: "Here, as too often in this great poem, that which is and may be known, but cannot *appear* from the given point of view, is confounded with the visible. It is no longer a mask-figure, but the character, of a Dissembler."[33] The whole point of dissemblance, Coleridge suggests, is that one cannot tell the hair is borrowed. But this apparent confusion of descriptive with thematic information leads Coleridge to another and, for our purposes, more crucial example: "Another common fault in stanza xvi: Grief represents two incompatibles, the grieved and the aggriever." Editor T. M. Raysor supplies the following lines, as misprinted by Anderson:

> Grief all in sable sorrowfully clad,
> Downe hanging his dull head with heavy chere;
> . . . . .
> A pair of pincers in his hand he had,
> With which he pinched many people to the hart.

"Indeed," Coleridge concludes, "this confusion of agent and patient occurs so frequently in his allegorical personages that

Spenser seems to have deemed it within the laws and among the legitimate principles of allegory." As occurs often in Coleridge, prescriptive criticism turns into descriptive insight; there is a note of fascination, as well as impatience, in this discovery of the figure's double relation to its idea. His choice of example is thematically as well as stylistically right. Kant's account of fanaticism shows why a brooding, fixating passion warrants a figure turned against itself; one thinks of Spenser's Despair, Milton's Sin, the figures ranged before the jaws of Virgil's hell, and virtually all the personifications the eighteenth century called "sublime." Even the word "passion" captures the paradox of Coleridge's "agent and patient." Kant's fanatic suffers from "an undermining disease"; the passion's real object and final victim is itself.[34] Although most personifications are, like Dissemblance, identified with themes they express to the point of descriptive absurdity, the personified passion is especially self-referential and self-enclosed. This trait again confirms the analogy with the fanatic; unlike the enthusiast, whose energies, owing to the negativity of the ideal, are perpetually extroverted, the fanatic totally identifies the ideal object with the empirical faculty that pursues it.

A brief example will suggest that attending to the reflexiveness of personification might revise our ways of reading sublime poetry. To support her claim that eighteenth-century horror-personifications derived their contemporary power and interest from "association with other manifestations of the supernatural," Patricia Meyer Spacks quotes the following lines from David Mallet's "The Excursion" (1728):

Behind me rises huge a reverend pile
Sole on his blasted heath, a place of tombs,
Waste, desolate, where Ruin dreary dwells.
Brooding o'er sightless sculls and crumbling bones,
Ghastful he sits, and eyes with stedfast glare
(Sad trophies of his power, where ivy twines
Its fatal green around) the falling roof,
The time-shook arch, the column grey with moss,
The leaning wall, the sculptur'd stone defac'd, . . .
All is dread silence here, and undisturb'd,

Save what the wind sighs, and the wailing owl
Screams solitary to the mournful Moon,
Glimmering her western ray through yonder isle,
Where the sad spirit walks with shadowy foot
His wonted round, or lingers o'er his grave.[35]

Next she cites, from a letter to Mallet, the response of James
Thomson (who, she notes, had apparently seen the lines "in a
slightly different form"):

You paint RUIN with a masterly Hand
   Gastful He sits, and views, *with* stedfast Glare,
   The falling Bust, the COLUMN grey *with* Moss
This is such an Attitude as I can never enough admire,
and even be astonished at.
   Save what the Wind sighs, and the WAILING OWL
   Screams solitary—
charmingly dreary!
   Where the *sad* Spirit walks, with *shadowy* Foot,
   His wonted Round, or lingers o'er his Grave.
What dismal Simplicity reigns thro these two lines!
They are equal to any ever Shakespear wrote on the
Subject.[36]

And Spacks comments:

   Even with due allowance made for friendship, the fact that
   Thomson chose to single out these lines for high praise suggests
   that for a contemporary audience they exercised a peculiar potency. Although the description of Ruin is not at all developed,
   depending on one line, Thomson finds it both admirable and
   astonishing. He praises his friend because he paints Ruin with
   a masterly hand, yet the fact is that Mallet paints Ruin almost
   not at all. Somehow, though, the effect of vivid personification
   is conveyed.

For Spacks, the rhetorical power here depends on "details" and
"associations," linking Ruin both to its actual effects in the world
and to a surrounding atmosphere of supernaturally tinted gloom.
The figure's vividness

   is conveyed through specific details about the physical surround-
   ings, details appropriate because they deal with the effects of
   ruin in the world of actuality, thus giving the personification firm

links with reality, but justified also merely by their "dismal Simplicity" and the "charmingly dreary" atmosphere they project.
The dreariness of the atmosphere, however, comes not primarily
from its physical details, but from its associations: the scene is
one in which ghosts might be expected to walk . . . Thus the
figure of Ruin comes to seem truly a supernatural personage . . . because he has been firmly placed in a supernatural context.[37]

No one familiar with Thomson's own poetry will doubt his
enjoyment of lurid atmosphere and conventional details, though
one might question whether the phrase "charmingly dreary"
bears out Spacks's claims for the "truly" supernatural impact of
Mallet's lines. More questionable, perhaps, is the claim that
skulls, ivy, arches, columns, and broken statues—the furniture
of countless allegorical paintings, recreated in countless gar-
dens—were meant to provide "firm links with reality."[38] But
the main question raised by Spacks's commentary is whether
such effects account for an interest in the personification itself.
In the one sentence specifically praising the personification,
Thomson emphasizes not the setting but the "Attitude" of the
figure. While attitude no doubt has primarily its pictorial sense
of posture or arrangement—older, according to the *Oxford English Dictionary,* than the psychological implication that entered
the language during exactly this period (ca. 1725)—Thomson's
sense of the pictorial here clearly includes the affective implications of "ghastful" and "glare." The glare is "stedfast" because
the personification is fixated on the effects of his own agency.
The striking peculiarity of Mallet's scene is not its stock treatment of a meditative landscape but its principal figure, for the
agent at the center of the ruins, instead of a poet, or saint, or
philosopher, is the brooding personification of Ruin itself. Is
"ghastful" Ruin here a ghost or aghast, agent or patient of his
own fanatic power? How genuine is the threat from a demon
who is self-enclosed in a conventional space, designed precisely
to express and enclose him? Ruin shares some of the stylized
impotence of the nearly comical "spirit" who sadly walks his
wonted round and lingers over his own grave. For the Enlightened poet and reader, such a figure gets its charm by perfectly
filling its alien and artificial space.

The Practice of Sublime Personification:
Collins' "Ode to Fear"

Few critics would bother to defend the psychological earnestness of Mallet's poetry. But Collins is another matter. Recently
a number of critics have drawn on psychoanalytic accounts of
Romanticism to affirm—or reaffirm—Collins' status as a serious
prophet of "daemonic" states of mind.[39] Such criticism shares
with more traditional accounts a tendency to distinguish Collins
sharply from his post-Augustan milieu and to align him with
such "visionary" figures as Milton and Blake. A serious challenge to what is becoming an orthodox view of Collins as a
solitary Romantic (or a Romantic Solitary) would require a fairly
detailed argument, ranging beyond the narrower issue of personification.[40] The following remarks, on Collins' fullest and
most explicit construction of an encounter between a poetic
speaker and a sublime personification, do not provide such a
challenge. But they do reflect a judgment that Collins stands at
the center, not the periphery, of eighteenth-century attitudes
toward poetic fiction, and that he shares the ambivalent interest
in figurative agency that we have found implicit in contemporary
accounts of personification. If Collins differs from his contemporaries, he does so mainly in the degree to which he consistently translates ambivalence toward poetry into poetic theme
and structure. Poems like "Ode to Fear" and "Ode on the Poetical Character" explicitly turn on an oscillating play between
identification with and insulation from representatives of archaic
poetic power (Fear in the former case, Fancy and Milton in the
latter).

In "Ode to Fear" the first aspect of sublime ambivalence,
identification, is almost embarrassingly stark. The poet identifies
with the personification to the point of compulsive mimicry
(5–8):

> Ah *Fear!* Ah frantic *Fear!*
> I see, I see Thee near.
> I know thy hurried Step, thy haggard Eye!
> Like Thee I start, like Thee disorder'd fly . . .[41]

Nowhere in Collins is the risk of literary fanaticism more obvious—a risk not of madness, as some earnest critics have as-

sumed, but of farce. Various commentators have noticed that the poet seems to trade places with his personification; what originated as the fictional externalization of his own emotion now leads him in a frantic mimetic dance. He becomes the patient as well as the agent of his invention, and therefore exhibits the fanatic reflexiveness of a sublime personification— a condition, however, for which he lacks the personification's ontological excuse.

The poet's reflexiveness, like his disordered flight, is in fact modeled on that of Fear, who is an "appall'd" spectator of scenes she has herself "inspir'd" (3, 43).[42] But the logic of reflexive agency is perhaps more explicit when Fear makes a cameo appearance—this time as an inexperienced male artist, like Collins himself—in the final poem in the 1746 volume, "The Passions: An Ode for Music." Plainly a variation on Dryden's "Alexander's Feast" and similar pieces in honor of St. Cecilia, the poem opens with a tableau set "in early *Greece*."[43] In the first sixteen lines, a crowd of personified passions, attending a recital by a young musician, Music, are suddenly "fir'd, / Fill'd with Fury, rapt, inspir'd"; they snatch "her Instruments of Sound" (13–16),

> And as they oft had heard a-part
> Sweet Lessons of her forceful Art,
> Each, for Madness rul'd the Hour,
> Would prove his own expressive Pow'r.

Ten solos follow; the first performance, comically brief, belongs to Fear (17–20):

> First *Fear* his Hand, its Skill to try,
>   Amid the Chords bewilder'd laid,
> And back recoil'd he knew not why,
>   Ev'n at the Sound himself had made.

As Roger Lonsdale observes, "The idea of Fear or Dread being terrified at itself or its own activities can be traced back in English at least to Sackville's Induction to *A Mirror for Magistrates*."[44] Fear at one's own agency also appears in figures that are not themselves personifications of fear; along with other critics, Lonsdale finds the opening lines of a sonnet by Sidney particularly close to Collins' quatrain:

A Satyre once did runne away for dread,
  With sound of horne, which he him selfe did blow,
Fearing and feared thus from himselfe he fled,
  Deeming strange evill in that he did not know.[45]

The device is also used by Spenser: Archimago's transformations into various animals, including "a dragon fell," are so convincing "That of himselfe he oft for feare would quake, / And oft would flie away" (*Faerie Queene,* I.ii.10).[46]

When they are not essentially ludicrous, episodes of reflexiveness in Collins' sources are likely to be demonic. The description of Fear's reaction to his own agency—he "back recoil'd he knew not why"—contains a precise verbal echo of *Paradise Lost.* Satan, having alighted on Mt. Niphates "in prospect of *Eden*" (Argument, book IV), is about to undertake (IV.15–18)

        his dire attempt, which nigh the birth
Now rolling, boils in his tumultuous breast,
And like a devilish Engine back recoils
Upon himself . . .

This, incidentally, is the moment at which Milton first explicitly enforces the allegorical identity between Satan and Hell ("for within him Hell / He brings, and round about him, nor from Hell / One step no more than from himself can fly"; 20–23)— an identity that Satan is soon compelled to acknowledge: "myself am Hell" (75).

Readers of Collins and his contemporaries will recognize the futility of trying to hold these writers thematically accountable for all their borrowings. Their poems are largely constructed out of quotations; the style depends on an irreverent freedom to yoke together phrases from a range of texts bearing little thematic relation to each other or to the subject at hand. The verbal link between Fear in "The Passions" and Milton's Satan may be no more than an accidental consequence of Collins' typical echolalia. But another glance at the context of Fear's performance may suggest that a reminiscence of Satanic violence is not irrelevant to Collins' intention. Fear and his colleagues are, after all, usurpers, who have interrupted an innocent and legitimate performer and stolen her instruments. And the image of an intoxicated crowd surrounding and, in a sense, attacking a lone musician might evoke an episode that haunted Milton: the murder of Orpheus by the mob of Bacchantes whose "barbarous dissonance" overwhelmed his "Harp and Voice" (*PL,* VII.32–38). In fact, Collins' passions "snatch" Music's instruments "From the supporting Myrtles round" (11–12), a gesture that seems to mimic the Bacchantes, who attacked Orpheus with rocks and branches torn from the landscape around him.[47] If the Ovidian episode really does stand behind the initial tableau of "The Passions," then its violence has been muted in two ways: first, by the conversion of Orpheus and the Bacchantes into merely allegorical agents; and second, by the dispersion of the Bacchantes' united clamor and mob action into a series of individual, self-expressive performances.[48] But the translation of rebellious fanaticism into edifying allegory and private "enthusiasm" is not very different, after all, from what happens in *Paradise Lost* to Satan and his followers, once the futility of their rebellion has been exposed. The angels in Hell are a collection of rather helpless eccentrics, each expressing one or another demonic passion; the speeches of Moloch, Belial, and Mammon in book II amount to an allegorical débat among personified attitudes, no longer capable of practical application. Satan's own agency, despite the strictly limited efficacy that God allows it, is essentially self-enclosed: as we are constantly reminded, his violence "shall redound / Upon his own rebellious head" (III.85–86).

The isolation and self-destruction of rebellious impulses has an immediate relevance to Collins. Most of his odes—including "The Passions"—were probably composed in the months following the defeat of the Young Pretender's forces at Culloden on April 16, 1746; at least two ("Ode, Written in the beginning of the Year 1746" and "Ode to Mercy") were directly occasioned by the rebellion.[49] Whether or not this national crisis in any sense underlies the uprising of Music's allegorical audience, Collins' poetry consistently depends on the transformation of

potential violence into reflexive attitude. The price of this transformation is a risk of absurdity, especially when the reflexive
agent is the poet himself; his self-expressive performance is
likely to seem a safe but trivial consummation of a presumptuous
ambition. Professing amazement at his own allegorical invention, the poet of "Ode to Fear" seems to embrace the condition
that his predecessors ironically imposed on their demonic or
ludicrous agents.

To treat one's own invention as an external power, then, is
at worst the mark of a Satanic fanatic, at best a symptom of the
innocent vanity that tricks Milton's Eve into a brief infatuation
with her own watery image. Somewhere between these two
extremes—or perhaps worse than both of them—is the reflexive absurdity of a Swiftian Aeolist or a Popean dunce. The virtual
identity, in Augustan satire, of Satanic presumption, innocent
vanity, and extravagant poetic invention is strikingly exemplified
by an episode in the third book of *The Dunciad*. The poet Settle,
filling the prophetic role of Virgil's Anchises and Milton's Michael, summons the spirit of Dr. Faustus, recently active in a
series of popular farces. The sorcerer conjures a vision of the
sublime absurdities that crowd the contemporary English stage:

> All sudden, Gorgons hiss, and Dragons glare,
> And ten-horn'd fiends and Giants rush to war.
> Hell rises, Heav'n descends, and dance on Earth:
> Gods, imps, and monsters, music, rage, and mirth,
> A fire, a jigg, a battle, and a ball,
> 'Till one wide conflagration swallows all.
>   Thence a new world to Nature's laws unknown,
> Breaks out refulgent, with a heav'n its own:
> Another Cynthia her new journey runs,
> And other planets circle other suns.
> The forests dance, the rivers upward rise,
> Whales sport in woods, and dolphins in the skies;
> And last, to give the whole creation grace,
> Lo! one vast Egg produces human race.

This vision forms part of the education of Settle's poetic son
(Theobald or Cibber, respectively, in the poem's earlier or later
versions), who reacts with appropriate wonder:

Joy fills his soul, joy innocent of thought;
"What pow'r, he cries, what pow'r these wonders wrought?"
"Son; what thou seek'st is in thee! Look, and find
Each Monster meets his likeness in thy mind."[50]

Taken together, these analogues to the poet's reflexiveness might seem to make Collins the unwitting target of an elaborate satire—composed, as it were, by the whole tradition of his predecessors. A psychologically earnest (that is, Romantic) reading of Collins' intention can have, it seems to me, no other outcome. What precludes such a reading, however, is the fundamental artificiality both of the poet's reflexive attitude and of the personification he pretends to mimic. This artificiality is designed to protect him from the danger of Cibberian naiveté— as well as from a deeper form of fanaticism, whose source will emerge as we approach the poem's center.

The artificiality of Collins' Fear—both the emotion and the agent—is signalled in various ways. In *Odes on Several Descriptive and Allegoric Subjects,* "Ode to Fear" comes immediately after the first poem in the volume, "Ode to Pity." Both poems—as well as the third, "Ode to Simplicity"—contain allusions to Greek tragedy; Collins may have composed them while working on his projected translation of Aristotle's *Poetics.*[51] In any case, the Aristotelian doublet makes an unmistakable appearance within "Ode to Fear" (42–45):

O *Fear,* I know Thee by my throbbing Heart,
    Thy with'ring Pow'r inspir'd each mournful Line,
Tho' gentle *Pity* claim her mingled Part,
    Yet all the Thunders of the Scene are thine!

The quatrain returns to the reflexiveness of the passage quoted earlier: one knows Fear by fearing. But the emotion now seems antique, theatrical, literary. The mournful lines, as the previous two stanzas indicate, belong to Sophocles, just as the appropriate emotions were prescribed by Aristotle. Collins is following an ancient recipe in an attempt to reconstitute an ancient experience. The goddess he invokes is not quite his own invention after all.

But the goddess may not be as ancient as she seems. The last

line verges on contemporary satire of the sort exemplified by
Cibber's vision of the stage. Roger Lonsdale detects "a curious
unconscious echo in this line of Pope, *Prologue for Mr. Dennis*
16: 'And shook the stage with Thunders all his own.' Pope was
referring to Dennis's invention of an improved method of making stage-thunder, a meaning C[ollins] would hardly wish to
include, if he was aware of it."[52] By now we may feel less confident than Lonsdale that the echo should be dismissed. Dennis
was not just an enemy of Pope, but a notorious early cham-
pion of the sublime, and artificial thunder, I have been argu-
ing, is what the sublime was (consciously and deliberately) all
about.

Stage-thunder is in fact entirely appropriate to the theatrical
character of the ode as a whole.[53] The word "scene"—always,
in Collins, with theatrical connotations—occurs three times in
this poem.[54] On the first occasion (line 3) its implicit fictionality
is rendered emphatically (even tautologically) explicit by the
adjective "unreal" (1–6):

> Thou, to whom the World unknown
> With all its shadowy Shapes is shown;
> Who see'st appall'd th' unreal Scene,
> While Fancy lifts the Veil between:
> Ah *Fear!* Ah frantic *Fear!*
> I see, I see Thee near.

The "unreal Scene" is simultaneously a fanatic hallucination,
which appalls the goddess because she mistakes it for reality;
an imaginary drama, staged by the impresario Fancy; and the
literal stage of classical tragedy. Fear, who begins as a spectator,
suddenly finds herself on stage, where she becomes the unwilling leader of a parade of allegorical monsters (7–25):

> I know thy hurried Step, they haggard Eye!
> Like Thee I start, like Thee disorder'd fly,
> For lo what *Monsters* in thy Train appear!
> *Danger,* whose Limbs of Giant Mold
> What mortal Eye can fix'd behold?
> Who stalks his Round, an hideous Form,
> Howling amidst the Midnight Storm,
> Or throws him on the ridgy Steep

Of some loose hanging Rock to sleep:
And with him thousand Phantoms join'd,
Who prompt to Deeds accurs'd the Mind:
And those, the Fiends, who near allied,
O'er Nature's Wounds, and Wrecks preside;
Whilst *Vengeance,* in the lurid Air,
Lifts her red Arm, expos'd and bare:
On whom that rav'ning * Brood of Fate,
Who lap the Blood of Sorrow, wait;
Who, *Fear,* this ghastly Train can see,
And look not madly wild, like Thee?

The tragic stage, as populated by these monsters, is curiously empty of what should stand at its center: tragic agency, the deed of horror. Like Mallet's Ruin, Danger and Vengeance are isolated, self-enclosed figures whose only function is theatrical display. Both lack victims. Danger merely "stalks his Round," not his prey; he circumscribes and fills a space which no one else seems in danger of entering. The potential violence of the verb "throws" is almost comically muted, after a teasing hint of disaster, by the infinitive that completes it: "to sleep." The emphasis of the description of Vengeance's arm falls not on its bloodiness (merely "red") but on its exhibition, "exposed and bare."⁵⁵ Even the striking depiction of the Furies as "that rav'ning Brood of Fate / Who lap the Blood of Sorrow" is interrupted by an asterisk (given above in its original position), which refers the reader to a scholarly note on the *Electra.*

The passage, in short, announces its politeness in ways that seem designed to prevent the reader from confusing Collins' artificial vision with the naive enthusiasm of its Cibberian equivalent. The poet's learned emotion begins on a level four or five times removed from its ostensible source, the archaic deed of horror: the poet imitates Fear, who sees the unreal scene, provided Fancy unveils it; and the scene itself is only a tableau of personifications, derived in turn from the incidents of classical tragedy, derived (according to Aristotle) from actual events. Collins' imitation of his own personified emotion is thus inserted into a sequence of mimetic relations that prevents the attribution of decisive agency to any particular agent and thus keeps the circle of reflexiveness from closing.

If this were as far as the poem went, we might safely dismiss it as an academic exercise, deftly skirting the edges of self-satire. But the narrative middle section of the ode (the mesode or, as Collins inaccurately labels it, the epode) suggests that more than urbanity is at stake in this complex shifting of identifications and differences. After a stanza on Fear's special popularity in Greece and another on Aeschylus' patriotism, Collins gives eight remarkable lines on Sophocles (34–41):

> But who is He whom later Garlands grace,
>> Who left a-while o'er *Hybla's* Dews to rove,
> With trembling Eyes thy dreary Steps to trace,
>> Where Thou and *Furies* shar'd the baleful Grove?
>
> Wrapt in thy cloudy Veil th' *Incestuous Queen*
> Sigh'd the sad Call her Son and Husband hear'd,
> When once alone it broke the silent Scene,
>> And he the Wretch of *Thebes* no more appear'd.

The first stanza inserts the tragedian into one of his own plays, *Oedipus at Colonus,* the action of which takes place at the entrance to a grove dedicated to the Eumenides. Sophocles follows Fear to the grove in exactly the same way that Collins elsewhere tries (but fails) to follow Milton to "An *Eden,* like his own" ("Ode on the Poetical Character," 62).[56] The stanza thus humbly marks the difference between the ancient poet, led by Fear to the center of tragedy, and the modern poet, who imitates Fear by fleeing.

The humility disappears, however, in the second stanza, when Collins offers what can only be a radical and deliberate revision of Sophocles' play. The stanza alludes to the disappearance of Oedipus, as narrated by a messenger at the conclusion of *Oedipus at Colonus.* The old man and his daughters were embracing and weeping; Collins supplies, in a note and in Greek, a portion (lines 1622–1625) of the messenger's account of what happened next:

> But when they finally stopped,
> And no more sobs were heard, then there was
> Silence, and in the silence suddenly
> A voice cried out to him—of such a kind
> It made our hair stand up in panic fear . . .

The passage in Sophocles goes on,

Again and again the call came from the god:
"Oedipus! Oedipus! Why are we waiting?
You delay too long; you delay too long to go!"[57]

Collins has altered two crucial details: he translates the repeated calls in Sophocles into a "sad call" that sounded "once alone," and he attributes the call not to "the god," as in the original, but to Jocasta, Oedipus' mother and wife, who died at the close of *Oedipus the King*. As if to avoid any appearance of mere oversight, Collins provides a note identifying the queen as Jocasta. Although his notes ignore the fact that this is a revision, Collins' stanza implicitly explains the divergence between the messenger's account and his own: Jocasta was mistaken for the god because she was wrapped in Fear's "cloudy Veil."

Fear's exact role here is hard to specify. In one sense she reveals the tragic incident—at least she leads Sophocles to the "baleful Grove." At the same time, however, she prevents him from seeing what the grove really contains: the chilling, claustrophobic discovery that what waits for Oedipus across the void is not a god but the incestuous mother. What makes this vision dangerous is not, I think, its exposure of an unnameable desire; neither Collins nor Sophocles seems much embarrassed by the topic of incest as such.[58] Incest here is itself a figure: it stands for the compression of ordinary differences into an extreme and essentially reflexive identity. Oedipus, seeking the murderer of Laius, found only himself. Collins merely completes this ironic logic of self-circling agency by confronting Oedipus with Jocasta, the personification of his own origin and fate. No matter were he goes, Oedipus advances only toward himself, and the magnificent Theban trilogy thus collapses into a single fanatic gesture of self-assertion: Danger stalks his round. The multiple cries of the god resolve into the single sad call of Jocasta—a call that would indeed break the "scene," since it would stop the play from ever being written.

Fear, then, acts as a surrogate spectator. She allows the poet a mediated participation in fanatic agency, while blocking the total identification that would freeze him into the horror or absurdity of pure reflexiveness. This role becomes explicit in the third and final section of the ode, a playful, almost precious account of popular superstitions, obviously indebted to Shakespeare and to Milton's *L'Allegro*. The passage includes an odd petition that Fear grant the poet a strong enough belief in such fictions to prevent him from finding them actually true (53–63):

> Dark Pow'r, with shudd'ring meek submitted Thought
> Be mine, to read the Visions old,
> Which thy awak'ning Bards have told:
> And lest thou meet my blasted View,
> Hold each strange Tale devoutly true;
> Ne'er be I found, by Thee o'eraw'd,
> In that thrice-hallow'd Eve abroad,
> When Ghosts, as Cottage-Maids believe,
> Their pebbled Beds permitted leave,
> And *Gobblins* haunt from Fire, or Fen,
> Or Mine, or Flood, the Walks of Men!

These lines clearly anticipate a poem unpublished in Collins' lifetime, the "Ode on the Popular Superstitions of the Highlands of Scotland, Considered as the Subject of Poetry" (written in 1749 or 1750). There Collins frankly urges a Scottish friend to exploit the "false themes" of his country's "rural faith" for the sake of artificial terror, just as "Shakespeare's Self with ev'ry Garland crown'd / In musing hour his Wayward Sisters found / And with their terrors drest the magic Scene!" (172, 32, 176–178). But this program seems less straightforward and complacent in the earlier ode. The suspension of disbelief inspired by Fear is more than a means of expanding the materials of poetic spectacle; it protects the poet from having his vision "blasted" by a return to literal belief—protects him, that is, from the condition of Oedipus, who was blinded by the discovery of an identity he thought he had left behind.[59]

This said; againe upon his Image gaz'd;
Teares on the troubled water circles rais'd:
The motion much obscur'd the fleeting shade.

Ovid, *Metamorphoses,* III.474–476,
translated by George Sandys (1626)

4 Wordsworth and the Limits of Allegory

Quasi-Personification in the "Intimations Ode"

The foregoing argument may help to explain both the (temporary) popularity of sublime personification and the relative failure of its *deliberate* practice. (The stress on "deliberate" is crucial here: personifications in Milton, Spenser, and Virgil were produced without the benefit of eighteenth-century notions of the sublime.) Powerfully concentrated—but also harmlessly enclosed—in the reflexive space of its own allegorical agency, the sublime personification was an ideal answer to the Enlightenment's ambivalence toward alien belief and archaic literature. But the very combination of qualities that makes the figure an ideal solution to a theoretical paradox—the desire for simultaneous identification with and dissociation from an image of "fanatical" power—at the same time deprives it of all but a momentary illusion of success. Both the attractive power and the overt fictionality of the personification derive from its "absorption" in its own allegorical meaning.[1] Yet fictionality within a poem is a relative effect; it depends on the isolation of the fictional agent from those other agents, including the poetic speaker, with which its fictionality is implicitly contrasted. The poet who fails or refuses to insulate the personification from contact with less overtly fictional agents invites the leveling effect deplored by critics of Milton's Sin and Death, while the poet who succeeds must give up the illusion of a genuinely threatening encounter. If the former replaces the sublime with allegory proper, the latter collapses into rhetorical posturing. The relative inadequacy of twentieth-century accounts of eighteenth-century sublime poetry may reflect the difficulty in deciding when a given poem has succumbed to which danger, as well as the frequent suspicion that it has managed to fall prey to both. This splitting apart of the sublime into its antithetical components may be exactly the effect cultivated by an antisublime performance such as *The Dunciad,* with its vertiginous oscillation between depictions of genuine fanatic self-absorption and of calculating hypocrisy. If a poet like Collins avoids such oscillation, he does so partly by signalling his awareness of how close that danger lies.[2]

It may be that major poetry could not be written in the sublime personifying mode, at least until the submergence of poetic ambivalence in its explicit eighteenth-century form. An alternative to the practical antinomies of sublime personification was devised by Wordsworth, who replaced the formal personifications of the eighteenth century with such quasi-allegorical but ostensibly natural figures as the Leech-Gatherer, the Discharged Soldier, the Blind Beggar, and the Philosopher-Child in the "Intimations Ode."[3] The preternatural self-enclosure of such figures comes closest to the abstract and formal reflexiveness of sublime personification in the encounter with the Blind Beggar, whose identity is wholly absorbed by the inscription he literally wears around his neck:

>   . . .'twas my chance
> Abruptly to be smitten with the view
> Of a blind beggar, who, with upright face,
> Stood propped against a wall, upon his chest
> Wearing a written paper, to explain

The story of the man, and who he was.
My mind did at this spectacle turn round
As with the might of waters, and it seemed
To me that in this label was a type
Or emblem of the utmost that we know
Both of ourselves and of the universe,
And on the shape of this unmoving man,
His fixèd face and sightless eyes, I looked
As if admonished from another world.[4]

By partially naturalizing the role that an eighteenth-century poet would unhesitatingly have assigned to a fully allegorical agent, Wordsworth allows his sublime figures to inhabit the same narrative or discursive space as the poet himself. Yet the resulting loss of an urbane and skeptical distance from such images of fanatical self-absorption disturbed even Coleridge, whose notorious attack on the eighth stanza of the "Intimations Ode" can be viewed as a refusal to accept Wordsworth's ambiguous naturalization of allegory. As the last example in his list of Wordsworth's "characteristic defects," Coleridge gives the following lines from the poet's apostrophe to the emblematic Child:

Thou best philosopher who yet dost keep
Thy heritage! Thou eye among the blind,
That, deaf and silent, read'st the eternal deep,
Haunted for ever by the Eternal Mind—
Mighty Prophet! Seer blest!
On whom those truths do rest,
Which we are toiling all our lives to find!
Thou, over whom thy immortality
Broods like the day, a master o'er the slave,
A presence that is not to be put by![5]

The general defect these lines are meant to exemplify is "an approximation to what might be called *mental* bombast, as distinguished from verbal: for, as in the latter there is a disproportion of the expressions to the thoughts, so in this there is a disproportion of thought to the circumstance and occasion" (*BL,* II, 136). In the case of this stanza, however, the "disproportion" takes the particularly interesting form of a dislocation of consciousness. Coleridge can make no literal sense of imputing *that* sort of consciousness to *that* sort of agent: "In what sense is a child of that age a *philosopher?* In what sense does he *read* 'the eternal deep?' In what sense is he declared to be '*for ever haunted* by the Supreme Being? or so inspired as to deserve the splendid titles of a *mighty prophet, a blessed seer?* By reflection? by knowledge? by conscious intuition? or by *any* form or modification of consciousness?' " (*BL,* II, 138). But an attempt to read the passage without imputing such consciousness to the Child proves equally futile, for "if these mysterious gifts, faculties, and operations, are *not* accompanied with consciousness; who *else* is conscious of them? or how can it be called the child, if it be no part of the child's conscious being?" Coleridge nevertheless experiments with two figurative readings. Perhaps the imputation of sublime consciousness to the Child only stands for the pantheist claim that every individual existence partakes of universal Spirit; but in that case the Child's "magnificent attributes" would be "equally suitable to a *bee,* or a *dog,* or a *field of corn* . . . The omnipresent Spirit works equally in *them,* as in the child; and the child is equally unconscious of it as they." The second figurative reading is suggested by four lines that Wordsworth later omitted but that originally followed immediately after the passage quoted above:

> To whom the grave
> Is but a lonely bed without the sense or sight
> Of day or the warm light,
> A place of thought where we in waiting lie.

"Surely," Coleridge remarks, "it cannot be that this wonder-rousing apostrophe is but a comment on the little poem of 'We are seven?' " Such a reading would translate the Child's consciousness of immortality into the mere incapacity of imagining death, an incapacity he would share with "all finite beings alike, of whatever age, and however educated or uneducated." In short, Coleridge concludes, Wordsworth's apostrophe has only the force of every specious paradox: "Thus it is with splendid paradoxes in general. If the words are taken in the common sense, they convey an absurdity; and if, in contempt of diction-

aries and custom, they are so interpreted as to avoid the absurdity, the meaning dwindles into some bald truism. Thus you
must at once understand the words *contrary* to their common
import, in order to arrive at any *sense;* and *according* to their
common import, if you are to receive from them any feeling
of *sublimity* or *admiration*" (*BL,* II, 139–141).

The antinomy of sense and nonsense that Coleridge describes
is strikingly parallel to the structure of the sublime in general:
in both cases the desired effect depends on taking literally what
is really an ingenious substitution. Rightly understood, the occasion turns banal. In that sense the sublime is always involved
in "mental bombast." But the fact that the paradox in this case
concerns a figurative imputation of consciousness takes us from
the general theory of the sublime to the specific practice of
sublime personification. The personification is a perfect emblem
of self-consciousness because its consciousness merely repeats
its allegorical identity. Personifications "know" only the abstractions they designate: Ruin knows only ruin. While the agency
of a personification need not be wholly reflexive—Ruin ruins
buildings and empires—the consciousness of a personification
typically is. A personification that knows more than its own
identity is already deviating from its allegorical role.

In personification, then, self-consciousness is imputed to a
figurative agent. But what happens when self-consciousness is
figuratively imputed to a *natural* agent, as in the case of Wordsworth's Child?[6] The imputation of an unnatural mode or degree
of consciousness has the effect of isolating the agent from its
natural context and thus of moving it closer to the condition of
a personification—without, however, assigning it a clear allegorical identity. It seems impossible to read the Child as a
personification of, say, immortality, or even of childhood. But
the Child's self-consciousness, precisely because it lacks both
natural explanation and rhetorical justification, produces an effect of isolated self-enclosure analogous to the stylized reflexiveness of explicit allegory.

There is much in the stanza to suggest that the Child is in
fact a modified version of an eighteenth-century sublime personification. The structure of the apostrophe itself, beginning

with the first two lines (omitted by Coleridge)—"Thou, whose exterior semblance doth belie / Thy Soul's immensity"—depends on the formulaic repetition of an emphatic "Thou," followed three times by a relative clause:

> Thou, whose exterior semblance doth belie . . .
> Thou best Philosopher, who yet dost keep . . .
> Thou, over whom thy Immortality
> Broods . . .

The sheer formality and insistent recurrence of this device already give the stanza an extravagant rhetorical heightening, especially after the rather awkward comedy of the preceding stanza. The formula itself is specifically reminiscent of Collins. Of the twelve poems in *Odes on Several Descriptive and Allegoric Subjects,* five begin with exactly this device: the odes to Pity ("O Thou, the Friend of Man assign'd"), to Simplicity ("O Thou by *Nature* taught"), to Mercy ("O Thou, who sit'st a smiling Bride"), to Peace ("O Thou, who bad'st thy Turtles bear"), and, most strikingly, to Fear:

> Thou, to whom the World unknown
> With all its shadowy Shapes is shown;
> Who see'st appall'd th' unreal Scene,
> While Fancy lifts the Veil between . . .[7]

Here the stylistic parallel is reinforced by a thematic one: both Wordsworth and Collins apostrophize an agent who is absorbed in the perception of a vision concealed from the poet himself.

The allegorical suggestions of this possible echo of Collins are further supported by the Child's reflexive brooding, as well as his participation in an emblematic tableau:

> Thou, over whom thy Immortality
> Broods like the Day, a Master o'er a Slave . . .

Coleridge objects in passing to the impropriety "of making a 'master *brood* o'er a slave,' or the *day* brood *at all*" (*BL,* II, 138); whatever the precise sense of these lines, they suggest at least a tendency toward a dramatic grouping of personified abstractions. In fact, however, the opacity of these metaphors—the impossibility of translating them into a literal argument despite the strong impression that they ought to be so translated, or of actually visualizing the tableau they suggest—precisely this double opacity thwarts their full allegorization. The semantic and, tonal ambiguity of "broods" (benevolently nurtures or moodily contemplates?) is not clarified but rather repeated by the crossed allegorical signals of the simile likening Immorality first to the day, then to a taskmaster. Allegorical tendencies are further hindered by the implied identification of the Child with the poet's own recollected infancy. A thorough allegorization of the Child—as a personification, for instance, of our desire for immortality—would have the indirect consequence of allegorizing the poet himself, and thus of converting the entire ode into an allegorical vision in the mode of a medieval dream-poem. (Wordsworth's own much later remarks on the poem do nothing to resolve the ambiguity; they assert both that the consciousness of immortality was a literal memory of the poet's own past, and that the Child's recollection of pre-existence was a merely figurative device for treating what Wordsworth now ponderously calls "the 'Immortality of the Soul,'" *PWW*, IV, 463–464.)

Wordsworth's partial or ambiguous allegorization of natural agents prevents the confident sorting out of literal and figurative intentions. In the context of the present argument it is hard not to view this effect as a lyric or discursive equivalent to the narrative mixing of literal and figurative agents that so disturbed eighteenth-century readers of *Paradise Lost*. The mixing of agents in Milton may reflect a pre-Enlightenment indifference to the maintenance of empirical consistency, but there is some evidence that Wordsworth may have deliberately cultivated the same effect as an essential token of the (for him) central tradition of the Hebraic imagination, consisting chiefly of Milton, Spenser, and the Bible. Rather than simply repudiating all allegory, as the well-known attack on "poetic diction" might suggest, Wordsworth viewed indefinite allegory as a kind of Protestant antidote to the tyranny of sensuous form. "The grand storehouses of enthusiastic and meditative Imagination," he wrote in the 1815 Preface, of poetical, as contradistinguished from human and dramatic Imagination, are the prophetic and lyrical parts of the Holy Scriptures, and the works of Milton; to which I cannot forbear to add those of Spenser. I select these writers in preference to those of ancient Greece and Rome, because the anthropomorphitism of the Pagan religion subjected the minds of the greatest poets in those countries too much to the bondage of definite form; from which the Hebrews were preserved by their abhorrence of idolatry. This abhorrence was almost as strong in our great epic Poet, both from circumstances of his life, and from the constitution of his mind. However imbued the surface might be with classical literature, he was a Hebrew in soul; and all things tended in him towards the sublime.   (*PrW*, III, 34–35)

The contrast between Hebrew sublimity and classical beauty is of course utterly commonplace; similar remarks by Coleridge and Kant have been quoted in earlier chapters. Equally ordinary is the alignment of Milton on the Hebraic side. But Wordsworth goes on, more surprisingly, to include Spenserian allegory in the same opposition to idolatry. Most telling of all is Wordsworth's observation that Spenser practiced two modes of allegory, the personification of abstractions and what I have been calling the "allegorization" of ostensibly natural agents.[8] Wordsworth's special endorsement of the latter reads like a description of his own emblematic figures: "Spenser, of a gentler nature, maintained his freedom by aid of his allegorical spirit, at one time inciting him to create persons out of abstractions; and, at another, by a superior effort of genius, to give the universality and permanence of abstractions to his human beings, by means of attributes and emblems that belong to the highest moral truths and the purest sensations,—of which his character of Una is a glorious example" (*PrW*, III, 35).[9]

It would be a mistake to cite such remarks as evidence of a genuine return to Renaissance attitudes. Wordsworth shares with the eighteenth century an interest in the general phenomenon of personification, apart from questions of its specific usage, that would have baffled Milton or Spenser. But by endorsing the coexistence and exchangeability of literal and figurative agents in Spenserian allegory, Wordsworth signals the distance between his own poetics and the eighteenth-century interest in such static, formally isolated figures as Mallet's Ruin. Though sometimes equally static—even to the point of ominous fixation—Wordsworth's figures are deprived of the full allegorical formality that would locate them in a sharply delineated figurative space. It is precisely the dislocating power of allegory that he admires. In general, and to Coleridge's frequent distress, Wordsworth seems to have been less involved in the poetic ambivalence that drove Coleridge to seek a reconciling medium between the literal and the figurative, and that inspired the eighteenth-century interest in self-absorbed but overtly fictional agents.

Allegory and Self-Reference in "Resolution and Independence"

In naturalizing the allegorical personifications of the sublime ode, Wordsworth renders the interest of his sublime agents not less but more abstract. The submergence of formal allegory means that a figure no longer announces—for example, by a proper name like Fear—either its thematic content or its fictionality. Paradoxically, however, this obscuring of the figure's allegorical identity tends to emphasize the fact of allegorization as such. By failing or refusing to reveal their allegorical meanings, Wordsworth's partially allegorized agents draw attention to the imagination's impulse to allegorize; more exactly, the impulse to allegorize is made noticeable by its curious inappropriateness to the agents to which it is applied. Precisely the discrepancy between the agent's natural status and its sudden acquisition of a quasi-allegorical resonance thus becomes, for Wordsworth, a formal index of imaginative power.

This translation of discrepancy into a revelation of power is by no means unique to episodes involving naturalized personifications. The sublime in general, as Wordsworth practices it, depends on the recognition of some disparity between the mind's exertions and the objects in which its energies are invested. Wordsworth's sublime, like Kant's, is essentially differential: the mind sees an image of transcendence in the magnitude of a discrepancy between some natural phenomenon and the importance imputed to it, just as the precise measure of the "soul's immensity" is the degree to which its "exterior semblance" can be taken to "belie" it. In certain instances, such as the well-known translation of disappointment into exultation during a recollection of crossing Simplon Pass, Wordsworth almost perfectly enacts a familiar Kantian scenario: an experience of failure indirectly reveals the preternatural strength of desire and hope.[10] In more typical instances, Wordsworth goes beyond even the highly artificial pathos of Kantian ambivalence to suggest a formal, almost clinical registering of disparities. In these cases, the significance of the sublime discrepancy seems strangely independent of the supposition of anyone's actually experiencing it. The sublime is restricted to a wholly abstract or exemplary role.

Wordsworth's whole doctrine of the "spots of time," for example, depends on the detachment of certain images from whatever emotions first made them seem important. A boy (1805 *Prelude*, XI.344–388) reacts superstitiously to his father's death, which he mistakenly interprets as a magical retribution for his own eagerness to go home on a school vacation.[11] His superstitious excitement fixes in his memory the image of an ordinary landscape associated with his intense desire to go home. Years later, long after the superstition has worn off, he discovers that the image has outlived the emotions that gave it its original salience. It survives as an abstract emblem of the mind's excessive power—strictly, a power to delude itself. And this *doctrine* of the mind's power—rather than any present experience of such power—is what makes the image a source of consolation in times of imaginative poverty. An early version of *The Prelude* explicitly states this principle of permanence through detachment from context:

> I might advert
> To numerous accidents in flood or field,
> Quarry or moor, or 'mid the winter snows,
> Distresses and disasters, tragic facts
> Of rural history, that impressed my mind
> With images to which in following years

Far other feelings were attached—with forms
That yet exist with independent life,
And, like their archetypes, know no decay.
                               (1799, first part, 279–287)

The role of Wordsworth's naturalized personifications is closely analogous to that of his "spots of time," though the sources of the sublime disparity are different in the two cases. The temporal character of the spots makes them specially dependent on autobiographical narrative. A single spot is necessarily the product of at least two separate moments in the career of a single agent. Only in the tranquil perspective of a later moment can the unwarranted excitement of the original experience be recognized as an index of the mind's transcendence, through illusion, of natural circumstance. But this temporal gap between a moment of powerful delusion and a later moment of quiet knowledge is not essential to the Wordsworthian sublime. Sometimes—and most strikingly in episodes of naturalized personification—the gap between two moments is replaced by a curious lack of fit between two ways of perceiving a single object. In both versions of the Wordsworthian sublime, the discrepancy between two perceptions is taken to reveal the imagination's power, its freedom from the constraints of natural fact. It is tempting to identify this power with the poet's own agency, and thus to assimilate Wordsworth's sublime to the strategies of self-reflection we have examined in his predecessors. In Collins, for instance, sublime personification allowed the poet to stabilize his relation to the "fanatical" power of alien belief by simultaneously identifying with and marking his distance from overtly fictional surrogates of the self. A similar strategy of mediated self-reflection might seem to account for the way Wordsworth measures his present distance from earlier, more superstitious versions of himself, or from the various emblematic figures he encounters. In fact, however, Wordsworth is typically up to something else. The drama of identification and distance is subordinated, in most major instances, to an interest in the way the sublime encounter *fails* to yield a stabilizing image of the self. We have already seen how the differential structure of the spots of time tends to deflect attention away from the continuities of personal experience toward an abstract doctrine of transcendence. In the case of Wordsworth's quasi-allegorical agents, it is not even clear that credit for the discrepancy between nature and representation belongs to the perceiving mind. Credit continues to go to the "imagination"; in that sense Wordsworth's sublime continues to involve a version of the self-referential turn we have witnessed elsewhere. But the imagination itself becomes curiously autonomous or mobile; unlike Coleridge, Wordsworth shows little interest in tracing it to an empirical origin in the poet's psyche. In fact, the point of his sublime agents seems to lie in the way they resist involvement in a psychological allegory by shrugging off, evading, or otherwise frustrating whatever self-reflexive investment they seem to invite.

The recalcitrance of such figures is nowhere more evident than in the case of the Leech-Gatherer in "Resolution and Independence" (*PWW*, II, 235–240). The Leech-Gatherer's recalcitrance is rendered especially obvious by his ostensible role as a source of consolation, a role for which he seems strikingly unsuitable. He is a physical as well as thematic anomaly; he seems to fit neither the psychological designs of the poet who encounters him nor the landscape in which the encounter takes place. But the characteristics that isolate him from the poem's thematic and descriptive contexts also make him the emblem of an agency whose origins prove impossible to trace to any particular agent.

The Leech-Gatherer first appears a third of the way through the poem when he is noticed by the highly self-conscious poetic speaker, who has been anxiously meditating, in a suitably barren landscape, on the bleakness of his own financial prospects. Eventually the poet engages the Leech-Gatherer in a rather awkward conversation, but only after the stationary figure at last begins to move—an event preceded by the following four stanzas of description (stanzas 8–11, 50–77):

> Now, whether it were by peculiar grace,
> A leading from above, a something given,
> Yet it befell that, in this lonely place,
> When I with these untoward thoughts had striven,

Beside a pool bare to the eye of heaven
I saw a Man before me unawares:
The oldest man he seemed that ever wore grey hairs.

As a huge stone is sometimes seen to lie
Couched on the bald top of an eminence;
Wonder to all who do the same espy,
By what means it could thither come, and whence;
So that it seems a thing endued with sense:
Like a sea-beast crawled forth, that on a shelf
Of rock or sand reposeth, there to sun itself;

Such seemed this Man, not all alive nor dead,
Nor all asleep—in his extreme old age:
His body was bent double, feet and head
Coming together in life's pilgrimage;
As if some dire constraint of pain, or rage
Of sickness felt by him in times long past,
A more than human weight upon his frame had cast.

Himself he propped, limbs, body, and pale face,
Upon a long grey staff of shaven wood:
And, still as I drew near with gentle pace,
Upon the margin of that moorish flood
Motionless as a cloud the old Man stood,
That heareth not the loud winds when they call;
And moveth all together, if it move at all.

The Leech-Gatherer appears as "something given," given presumably to the poet as a means of calming his fears of "Solitude,
pain of heart, distress, and poverty" (35). In an earlier version
(before 1820) of stanza 8, there is a suggestion that the Old
Man's function will be to stabilize the violent mood-swings re-
counted in the preceding stanzas; the poet says that the vision
occurred "When up and down my fancy thus was driven, / And
I with these untoward thoughts had striven" (*PWW*, II, 237 app.
crit.). Despite these signals, which seem designed to locate the
Old Man in the poem's psychological and phenomenological
setting, the actual description makes it extremely hard to specify
his relation to the perceiver.

How and where, for instance, is the Old Man located in the
landscape with which the descriptive similes might seem to

identify him? The protagonist sees a Man before him, but at what distance and at what angle? If the Old Man resembles a huge stone on the top of an eminence, then presumably the speaker is looking uphill at a distant object. But a sea-beast can only crawl forth at sea level, which suggests that the Old Man is at, or more likely below, the speaker's own elevation. The sea-beast, moreover, has an obvious origin—namely, the sea— and an obvious means of arrival—namely, crawling forth. But the stone amazes all its viewers, who wonder "By what means it could thither come, and whence." This ambiguity about the Old Man's mode of arrival applies as well to the speaker's mode of discovery: should we assume that the speaker's perception took the form of sudden or of gradual recognition? "I saw a Man before me unawares"—is "unawares" an adverb modifying the speaker's action ("I saw him unexpectedly") or an adjective indicating the Old Man's obliviousness of—or indifference to— the speaker?

Wordsworth's own analysis of the description in his 1815 Preface ignores such questions of location and focuses instead on what might be called the Old Man's ontology. What I have been describing as an ambiguity in the figure's spatial and phenomenological relation to the poetic speaker interests Wordsworth here as an ambiguity in the Old Man's degree of agency, and thus as a symptom of the imagination's capacity to manipulate what Wordsworth calls "the indications of life and motion." In the double simile of stanza 9, according to Wordsworth,

> the conferring, the abstracting, and the modifying powers of the Imagination, immediately and mediately acting, are all brought into conjunction. The stone is endowed with something of the power of life to approximate it to the sea-beast; and the sea-beast stripped of some of its vital qualities to assimilate it to the stone; which intermediate image is thus treated for the purpose of bringing the original image, that of the stone, to a nearer resemblance to the figure and condition of the aged Man; who is divested of so much of the indications of life and motion as to bring him to the point where the two objects unite and coalesce in just comparison. (*PrW*, III, 33)

The technical point of this analysis seems clear enough: the effect of coalescence results from a series of parallel adjustments in degrees of agency. But what, if anything, is the thematic point of the imagination's procedure? Is the simile, for instance, a way of reconciling human life and inanimate nature, in which case it might indeed provide an emblematic response to the poet's fears of hyperconscious isolation and material poverty? The trouble with such an account is that the figurative coalescence in this stanza does not seem to reconcile humanity and nature but instead to isolate the terminal images, Old Man and stone, from their respective origins in human life and mineral lifelessness. The simile, like the Leech-Gatherer himself in stanza 10, is not so much a reconciliation of life and death as an anomalous negation of both conditions—"not all alive nor dead"—and the simile's effect, a kind of centripetal isolation, is matched by the way the Old Man is "bent double, feet and head / Coming together in life's pilgrimage."

These observations on the peculiarity of the Leech-Gatherer's location and status already indicate the difficulty of establishing his precise relation to the context of the protagonist's self-conscious meditation. Something like a thematic connection seems to emerge, however, when the Old Man eventually begins to move, in the stanza following the description (stanza 12, 78–81):

> At length, himself unsettling, he the pond
> Stirred with his staff, and fixedly did look
> Upon the muddy water, which he conned,
> As if he had been reading in a book . . .

A figure in this attitude is supposed to be looking at his or her own image, like Milton's Eve, who remembers lying down beside a lake, the moment after her creation (*PL,* IV.456–462),

> to look into the clear
> Smooth Lake, that to me seem'd another Sky.
> As I bent down to look, just opposite,
> A Shape within the wat'ry gleam appear'd
> Bending to look on me, I started back . . .

Wordsworth's variations on this Ovidian motif are of course endless, but two instances seem especially close to the Leech-

Gatherer's fixed gazing into the pond. When Peter, in *Peter Bell* (*PWW*, II, 331–382), suddenly glimpses a drowned man's corpse beneath the waters of the River Swale, the narrative explodes into a grotesquely comic series of hypothetical explanations of his terror. The narrator mentions—but only in passing—the possibility that Peter has merely seen his own reflection (501–505):

> Is it the moon's distorted face?
> The ghost-like image of a cloud?
> Is it a gallows there portrayed?
> Is Peter of himself afraid?
> Is it a coffin,—or a shroud?

The list goes on through a series of increasingly Gothic possibilities, including, in a notorious stanza that Wordsworth removed after people were appalled by the first published version in 1819, the image of "a party in a parlour,"

> Cramm'd just as they on earth were cramm'd
> Some sipping punch, some sipping tea,
> But, as you by their faces see,
> All silent and all damn'd!   (*PWW*, II, 354 app. crit.)

The episode is clearly a violent parody of self-reflexive gazing: one's own image is merely one of a series of possible occasions for a pointless theatrical terror, an occasion possessing no more or less personal interest than the actual source of Peter's vision, the corpse, which Peter will soon extract from the river by winding his staff in its hair.[12] The relevance of this episode of skewed and trivialized narcissism to the figure of the Leech-Gatherer becomes clear when Peter's gaze, like the Leech-Gatherer's, is compared to an act of reading (516–520):

> Never did pulse so quickly throb,
> And never heart so loudly panted;
> He looks, he cannot choose but look;
> Like some one reading in a book—
> A book that is enchanted.

In *Resolution and Independence*, Peter's Gothic inability to "read" himself—or any particular meaning—in the river into which he can't help gazing appears in a strangely attenuated and undramatic form. The lines, once again:

> At length, himself unsettling, he the pond
> Stirred with his staff, and fixedly did look
> Upon the muddy water, which he conned,
> As if he had been reading in a book . . .

The Old Man "unsettles" himself in two ways: by moving his body and by disturbing his image, which is presumably reflected by the motionless surface of the pond before he stirs it. And it is only after he stirs up its muddy bottom that he begins to read the pond—searching, of course, not for any image of the self but for tiny, wriggling leeches—increasingly hard to find, as we know from Dorothy's detailed account of her and William's meeting with the actual Leech-Gatherer.[13] If this is narcissism, it is narcissism in an oddly minimal form, reduced to a kind of technical scanning for miniature blips in a virtually opaque medium.

The miniaturization of what ought to serve as images of the self is also characteristic of *The Thorn* (*PWW*, II, 240–248), which was written immediately before the first version of *Peter Bell* in the spring of 1798. Toward the end of this poem the narrator either reports or imagines the result of gazing into the pond that lies a few yards distant from the thorn itself (214–220):

> Some say, if to the pond you go,
> And fix on it a steady view,
> The shadow of a babe you trace,
> A baby and a baby's face,
> And that it looks at you;
> Whene'er you look on it, 'tis plain
> The baby looks at you again.

This time the joke seems to be the opposite of the grisly one in *Peter Bell:* what the narrator or his source has seen in the pond is obviously his own reflection and not an actual corpse. Gothic horror reverts to unconscious narcissism. But what are we to make, in that case, of the curious oscillation between the baby and the baby's face? Has the viewer seen what he thought was a baby's face—but was in fact his own face—and only imagined a baby's body to go with it? Or is the entire image, body and face together, required to match the size of an adult countenance?

This lack of a satisfactory fit between the self and what is supposed to reflect it extends to the strange little cluster of images—the thorn, the pond, the mossy heap, and Martha Ray herself—that seem huddled together in an otherwise vast and empty landscape. Introduced one by one over the course of six stanzas, these objects are arranged, or more exactly deposited, in a space beginning no more than five yards, the narrator tells us, from the mountain path from which one "espies" them (27–28). The closest object, the tree, is "Not higher than a two years' child" (5); next comes the "beauteous heap, a hill of moss," which is "like an infant's grave in size" (36, 52) and is "Just half a foot in height" (37). In lines that were present in the original version but removed after 1815, the narrator tells us that the farthest object, the "little muddy pond" (30), the site of the narcissistic gazing already discussed, is "three feet long, and two feet wide"—and he assures us that he has "measured it from side to side" (*PWW*, II, 241 app. crit.). Martha herself sits between the heap and the pond, which is located only "three yards beyond" the tree (29). Adding three feet for the length of the pond, and another foot or so for the diameter of the tree itself, gives a maximum extension of roughly thirteen feet for the entire scene. At one point in the poem the extreme disproportion between the cluster of images and the surrounding landscape is emphasized by a bizarre optical illusion that parallels the spatial ambiguities involving the Leech-Gatherer. The narrator recalls being caught in a fierce storm and seeking shelter beneath what he thought was a "jutting crag" (182); he ran (183–187)

> Head-foremost, through the driving rain,
> The shelter of the crag to gain;
> And, as I am a man,
> Instead of jutting crag, I found
> A Woman seated on the ground.

This neck-breaking double take is more dramatic, perhaps, than anything in "Resolution and Independence," but the thematic link seems clear. The narrator's desperate search for shelter parodies in advance the anxious poet's longing for what Coleridge would call a "companionable form" to assuage his fears of destitution. But the point of both episodes seems to be the almost ludicrous inappropriateness of an image that seems at first, by its very isolation, to offer itself as a response to the subject's wish. In both poems this pattern of deflected narcissism seems associated with spatial anomalies, including a peculiar miniaturization of whatever it is that is supposed to reflect the self.

Corresponding to the slipperiness or inadequacy of the central image in "Resolution and Independence" is the speaker's well-known but still mysterious inability to concentrate on what he himself wants to interpret as a providential answer to his needs. This is the point, of course, of Lewis Carroll's brilliant parody "The White Knight's Song," in which the speaker keeps asking an old man how he makes his living and then instantly lapses into reverie about his own self-interested schemes, thinking, for example,

> of a way
> To feed oneself on batter,
> And so go on from day to day
> Getting a little fatter.

Among the felicities in his version, Carroll brings out the social disparity implicit in the encounter: the gentleman poet finally pays attention when the old man obsequiously offers to "drink / Your Honour's noble health."

> I heard him then, for I had just
> Completed my design
> To keep the Menai bridge from rust
> By boiling it in wine.
> I thanked him much for telling me
> The way he got his wealth,
> But chiefly for his wish that he
> Might drink my noble health.[14]

Carroll's point is well taken: the Leech-Gatherer's "flash of mild surprise" (90) when the protagonist addresses him, like his mys-

terious smile several stanzas later (120), is at least partly accountable as a response to the rather forced chumminess of a
social superior. But the social awkwardness corresponds—and
indeed I think refers—to a very different kind of awkwardness
that, when examined, will suggest what the Leech-Gatherer really
stands for.

The speaker's attention actually lapses twice. On the first
occasion, the Leech-Gatherer has been recounting the simple
facts of his life and profession. His discourse is not quoted, but
its formal characteristics are described in some detail (92–
98):

> His words came feebly, from a feeble chest,
> But each in solemn order followed each,
> With something of a lofty utterance drest—
> Choice word and measured phrase, above the reach
> Of ordinary men; a stately speech;
> Such as grave Livers do in Scotland use,
> Religious men, who give to God and man their dues.

This descripion of the Old Man's style reads remarkably like a
description of the speaker's own discourse—or rather of the
poetic medium in which that discourse is fictionally expressed.
In fact, the Leech-Gatherer's speech, as the young poet describes it, seems more appropriate to the language of the poem's
slightly shortened Spenserian stanzas than does the poet's own
anxious meditation, which might be more suitable for the ir-
regular Pindarics of a "Dejection" or an "Intimations" ode. And
this impression is reinforced by the repetitive and alliterative
style of the indirect discourse in the next stanza (99–105):

> He told, that to these waters he had come
> To gather leeches, being old and poor:
> Employment hazardous and wearisome!
> And he had many hardships to endure:
> From pond to pond he roamed, from moor to moor;
> Housing, with God's good help, by choice or chance;
> And in this way he gained an honest maintenance.

It is at this point that the speaker records his first inexplicable
lapse into reverie, a condition accompanied by his inability to

perceive the stately divisions that mark the Old Man's speech
(106–112):

> The old Man still stood talking by my side;
> But now his voice to me was like a stream
> Scarce heard; nor word from word could I divide;
> And the whole body of the Man did seem
> Like one whom I had met with in a dream;
> Or like a man from some far region sent,
> To give me human strength, by apt admonishment.

But instead of consolation, the effect of this notion is only to
bring back the speaker's "former thoughts" of ruin, which lead
him to repeat his original question, " 'How is it that you live,
and what is it you do?' " (113–119). After a stanza in which the
Leech-Gatherer patiently rehearses his earlier account, the speaker
slides once again into reverie (127–133):

> While he was talking thus, the lonely place,
> The old Man's shape, and speech—all troubled me:
> In my mind's eye I seemed to see him pace
> About the weary moors continually,
> Wandering about alone and silently.
> While I these thoughts within myself pursued,
> He, having made a pause, the same discourse renewed.

This time the Old Man's pausing and renewing of the "same
discourse" is spontaneous: no question from the speaker has
intervened to break off his narrative and start it over. The
pattern of pausing and renewing has drifted away from its dramatic motivation, in the same way that the haunting image of
the wandering Leech-Gatherer has slipped free of the stationary
figure by the poet's side. In *Wordsworth's Poetry*, Geoffrey H.
Hartman devotes an intriguing paragraph to this production of
what he calls an after-image:

> An *after-image* of this kind plays an important role in many
> of Wordsworth's poems. It expresses the possibility of the re-
> newal (or at least recurrence) of a certain experience by including
> that possibility in the very structure of the experience. As a
> mental reflex, the after-image elongates the encounter, and as
> an image *of* something, it may also suggest an indefinitely ex-

tended action. Not any action, of course: it is the image, itself repeated, of a repeated and persistent action which moves the Leech-gatherer closer to the figure of the Wandering Jew and brings about Wordsworth's recognition of his firmness.[15]

"The image, itself repeated, of a repeated and persistent action"—this splendid formulation has built into it the key to what it is about the Leech-Gatherer that precisely evades the phenomenological—indeed, the *Coleridgean*—appropriation Hartman describes.[16] For what is it in fact that paces continually, laborious and opaque, across the field of the poet's and the reader's consciousness? What in this poem is marked by "Choice word and measured phrase, above the reach / Of ordinary men; a stately speech"? What is it that moveth altogether if it move at all; that repeatedly makes a pause and then the same discourse renews? What is it, finally, that in its antiquity, its persistence, and its self-enclosed indifference to any particular thematic content, is bound to evade the narcissistic strategies of an anxious Coleridgean poet who so desperately wants it to answer to his personal need?

Nothing else, it seems to me, but the condensed Spenserian stanza (measured, antique, opaque, elusive) whose persistent and finally pointless repetition constitutes this very poem. The Leech-Gatherer is nothing other than a materialized deposit, a kind of personified sediment or precipitate, of the stanzas that serve as the deliberately awkward and alien medium of the speaker's meditation. If the speaker's encounter with the Leech-Gatherer triggers a version of the self-referential turn that the sublime requires, the agency referred to is not a faculty in the speaker's own mind but whatever force it is—Wordsworth would say Imagination—that keeps the stanzas pacing in their halting but inexorable way. The speaker himself, after all, is only another effect of the same procedure of temporary condensation; he only enters the poem, as numerous readers have noticed, with the shift from description to narrative, and from present to past tense, at the beginning of the third stanza. Both figures are introduced to dramatize the disparity between the poetic medium and the strategy of self-reflection that elsewhere characterizes the sublime experience proper.[17]

The Leech-Gatherer's role as a figure standing for the autonomy of the poem's stanzas is related to the impression he gives of being thematically rich and flat at the same time. Beyond the odd resemblance he bears to a Spenserian stanza, he has descriptive affinities to a number of Spenserian characters—most strikingly perhaps to the disguised Archimago (*Faerie Queene*, I.i.29) and to Orgoglio's doorkeeper Ignaro (I.viii.30–34). But such affinities are complicated by the fact that he also reminds one of the mysterious old man in Chaucer's *Pardoner's Tale*, as well as of Satan in *Paradise Regained*, who shows up at the first temptation in an Archimago-like disguise (I.314). The multiplicity, contradictoriness, and vagueness of such affinities have the effect not so much of imbedding the Leech-Gatherer in a coherent thematic tradition as of reducing his relation to earlier poetry to a merely formal reminiscence.[18] The result is a peculiar sense that one is encountering a familiar character who is at the same time no more than a cipher for the very medium that makes him seem familiar. He becomes a personification of allegorical poetry, although his role as a figure for allegory in general depends on his lack of a clear relation to any particular allegorical meaning, or more exactly, to any particular allegorical meaning besides allegory itself. For Wordsworth's version of the sublime is no more or less thematic than the versions it simultaneously invokes and resists. The sublime continues to require the translation of discrepancy into a revelation of power. The Leech-Gatherer, like other sublime objects, both produces and represents a powerful discrepancy, specifically a discrepancy between psychological theme and poetic medium. The power thus indicated is not exactly God, or the self, or even the poet's own imagination. It is the power itself of poetic representation, conceived by Wordsworth as the repeated dislocation of attention from particular images of the self.

Personification Revisited: "Yew-Trees"

Taken together, the previous two sections suggest that on one hand, Wordsworth largely abandons the practice of explicit personification (thus jettisoning much of the self-conscious theatricality of a poet like Collins), while on the other other hand, he allows his sublime agents to retain enough of their allegorical heritage to prevent them from comfortably inhabiting their naturalized roles. The discrepancy between their naturalistic and allegorical tendencies, like the contrast between the successive moments constituting each "spot of time," provides a differential measure of imaginative power. But the imagination itself, as it operates on a figure like the Leech-Gatherer, is not so much a faculty of the individual mind as it is a recurrent pattern of attention and oblivion, of concentration and diffusion, produced by the agency of poetic form.

Although this interpretation fits such figures as the Child or the Leech-Gatherer, it may seem in need of revision when we consider a poem in which Wordsworth strikingly returned to formal personification, a practice he had generally left behind after his earliest poetry. A juvenile text like his fragment "The Vale of Esthwaite" (1787), indebted to sublime and Gothic passages in Milton, Gray, Collins, and James Beattie, is exuberantly populated by Superstition, Terror, Murder, Suicide, Madness, and various other "forms of Fear."[19] Explicit personification never completely disappears; Wordsworth's account of his Cambridge education in *The Prelude,* for example, includes an elaborate tableau of personifications acting out proverbial human foibles (1805, III.630–643).[20] The "Ode to Duty" is an extended apostrophe to a personified abstraction, although Duty herself never makes a visible appearance—is never brought on stage, as she would be, say, in Collins. On the whole, however, in the sublime episodes of the major poetry, personifications are replaced by the naturalized agents described above. The sudden reappearance of a cluster of personifications in a poem that is both sublime and major—"Yew-Trees" (composed in 1803 or later)—is consequently startling:

> There is a Yew-tree, pride of Lorton Vale,
> Which to this day stands single, in the midst
> Of its own darkness, as it stood of yore:
> Not loth to furnish weapons for the bands
> Of Umfraville or Percy ere they marched   5
> To Scotland's heaths; or those that crossed the sea

And drew their sounding bows at Azincour,
Perhaps at earlier Crecy, or Poictiers.
Of vast circumference and gloom profound
This solitary Tree! a living thing   10
Produced too slowly ever to decay;
Of form and aspect too magnificent
To be destroyed. But worthier still of note
Are those fraternal Four of Borrowdale,
Joined in one solemn and capacious grove;   15
Huge trunks! and each particular trunk a growth
Of intertwisted fibres serpentine
Up-coiling, and inveterately convolved;
Nor uninformed with Phantasy, and looks
That threaten the profane;—a pillared shade,   20
Upon whose grassless floor of red-brown hue,
By sheddings from the pining umbrage tinged
Perennially—beneath whose sable roof
Of boughs, as if for festal purpose decked
With unrejoicing berries—ghostly Shapes   25
May meet at noontide; Fear and trembling Hope,
Silence and Foresight; Death the Skeleton
And Time the Shadow;— there to celebrate,
As in a natural temple scattered o'er
With altars undisturbed of mossy stone,   30
United worship; or in mute repose
To lie, and listen to the mountain flood
Murmuring from Glaramara's inmost caves.[21]

(*PWW*, II, 209–210)

Nothing quite mitigates the surprise of encountering these ghostly abstractions (26–28), who seem to appear from nowhere, breaking the poem's train of thought as much as they complete it. But they are, nevertheless, prepared for by a series of earlier gestures toward personification. The Lorton Yew was "not loth" to contribute its limbs to medieval armies, and this modest hint of voluntary agency lends a degree of animation to other, ostensibly descriptive details.[22] The tree "stands single, in the midst / Of its own darkness"; it thus partakes of the reflexiveness of a personification like Mallet's Ruin (discussed in Chapter 3), who sits at the center of a space defined and encompassed by his own agency.[23] The combination of darkness, isolation, and magnificence may draw some of its energy from descriptions of epic giants. In particular, the phrases closing the description of the Lorton Yew—"Of form and aspect too magnicent / To be destroyed"—distantly echo one of Milton's descriptions of Satan, "In shape and gesture proudly eminent" above his followers when "his form had yet not lost / All her Original brightness, nor appear'd / Less than Arch-Angel ruin'd" (*PL*, I.589–593).

The poet's encounter with the solitary yew seems almost to trigger a process of reverse metamorphosis, as if Wordsworth in this poem were undoing his own transformation of explicit personifications into natural persons and objects. In the next phase of the poem, after the abrupt switch to the "fraternal Four of Borrowdale," this curious drive toward allegory seems to intensify.[24] By line 19, the coiling energy of the fibrous trunks has coalesced into the quasi-independent figure of Phantasy. But Phantasy remains, as it were, in bas-relief, only half detached from the shapes that suggest it. Those "looks / That threaten the profane" are not quite Phantasy's own looks; they, like Phantasy, still "inform" the serpentine trunks.

The exact sense in which Phantasy "informs" (more scrupulously, does "not uninform") the yews' trunks is obscure. Do the twisted fibers resemble the products of a fantastic artist? do they inspire the viewer to fantasize? or do they themselves possess a fantasizing consciousness? Precisely its ambiguous status *ought* to make Phantasy the decisive figure here, a saving intermediary between nature and consciousness, in accordance with the familiar Romantic program. But from that point of view, the poem's final turn—its production of explicit personifications, fully detached from organic ties to description—would seem worse than superfluous. Tracing the progression from nature to personification does not yet amount to explaining it.

One natural way to account for the personifications would be to view them as surrogates of an agent who otherwise seems strangely excluded from his own meditation: the poet himself. The assumption that these figures stand for the poet's (or speaker's) own engagement is, in fact, taken for granted in the two most elaborate readings the poem has received. Comparing "Yew-Trees" with more typical Wordsworthian lyrics, Michael Riffaterre remarks, "The listening subject is normally actualized in the person of the narrator. The difference in 'Yew-Trees' is of course that the narrator's thoughts, the ghosts, take his place as listener."[25] To Geoffrey H. Hartman, the supplanting of an explicit narrator by personifications reflects far more than an incidental variation on a typical structure: "The strong device of personification reveals a more inobvious and deeply sustaining figure. From the very beginning we must accept the voice that speaks as, somehow, akin to the Yew-tree itself in ghostly extension or longevity." The poem as a whole, and not just its conclusion, testifies to "that *imaginative transference* which is at the root of opposite yet related devices essential to poetry: impersonation (personification, animistic metaphor), on the one hand, and impersonal constructions eliding narrator or human intermediary on the other. Negation of self is, in both, accompanied by a magnified sense of the other which leads to mythic, archaic, or spectral symbols. The yews make a ghost of the speaker."[26] But this "negation of self" is not as austere or total as it sounds. "Elision" remains for Hartman a mode of implied presence: "the poet-medium" is really "there all the time." What the poet loses in explicit presence he gains in an implicit magnification of consciousness: "In so subtly eliding the human intermediary, Wordsworth evokes a state of consciousness directed toward a quasi-eternal object and proceeding from a quasi-eternal repose."[27] As in Kant's sublime, a secret identification overrides an overt alienation, and personification becomes an indirect way of preserving the poet's self.

Both Riffaterre and Hartman, then, see the personifications as authorized by their implied dependence on the poet's own agency. The trouble with this justification, however, is the lack of compelling grounds for supposing that the thoughts personified are in fact the poet's own. The thoughts, after all, are conventional passions, with all the blandness of figures in an eighteenth-century progress poem. But their presentation as a cluster of phantoms evinces a still more ancient and impersonal lineage.

Editors have long been aware of a resemblance between Wordsworth's figures and the horror personifications encountered by Aeneas and the Sybil at the threshold of Virgil's Hell in *Aeneid,* VI (273–281):

> Before the entrance, at the jaws of Orcus,
> both Grief and goading Cares have set their couches;
> there pale Diseases dwell, and sad Old Age,
> and Fear and Hunger, that worst counsellor,
> and ugly Poverty—shapes terrible
> to see—and Death and Trials; Death's brother, Sleep,
> and all the evil Pleasures of the mind;
> And War, whose fruits are death; and facing these,
> the Furies' iron chambers; and mad Strife,
> her serpent hair bound up with bloody garlands.[28]

Virgil's figures—who also happen to surround a dark, enormous elm (*ulmus opaca, ingens*), a nest for throngs of false dreams (282–284)—are only the first in a long succession of allegorical guardian-clusters familiar to Wordsworth. Spenser's Guyon encounters Payne, Strife, Revenge, Despight, Treason, Hate, Gealosie, Feare, Sorrow, Shame, Horrour, and the harpy Celeno, all collected "before the gates of *Pluto*" in the depths of Mammon's underworld (*Faerie Queen*, II.vii.21–22).[29] Like Wordsworth's enigmatic figures, Spenser's remain strangely silent, and Guyon's reaction is appropriate to the viewer of a sublime spectacle: he "with wonder all the way / Did feed his eyes, and fild his inner thought" (stanza 24).

In *Paradise Lost,* these Virgilian and Spenserian groups are condensed into a pair of infernal gatekeepers, Sin and Death, but a full cluster dramatically reappears at the close of Pope's *Windsor-Forest,* when Father Thames prophesies their banishment, by Peace, "from Earth to deepest Hell" (413, 414–422):

> In Brazen Bonds shall barb'rous *Discord* dwell:
> Gigantick *Pride,* pale *Terror,* gloomy *Care,*
> And mad *Ambition,* shall attend her there.
> There purple *Vengeance* bath'd in Gore retires,
> Her Weapons blunted, and extinct her Fires:
> There hateful *Envy* her own Snakes shall feel,
> And *Persecution* mourn her broken Wheel:

There *Faction* roar, *Rebellion* bite her Chain,
And gasping Furies thirst for Blood in vain.

Thirty years later, in 1743, Pope concluded the final version of his *Dunciad* with his astonishing vision of the triumph of Dulness. The passage includes a demonic reversal of the scene in *Windsor-Forest,* as a series of benevolent personifications flee, shrink, and expire before the dark goddess's "felt approach, and secret might" (IV.639, 641–650):

> See skulking *Truth* to her old Cavern fled,
> Mountains of Casuistry heap'd o'er her head!
> *Philosophy,* that lean'd on Heav'n before,
> Shrinks to her second cause, and is no more.
> *Physic* of *Metaphysic* begs defence,
> And *Metaphysic* calls for aid on *Sense!*
> See *Mystery* to *Mathematics* fly!
> In vain! they gaze, turn giddy, rave, and die.
> *Religion* blushing veils her sacred fires,
> and unawares *Morality* expires.[30]

If this passage is a reversal of the situation at the end of *Windsor-Forest,* it is also a revision of the episodes in Virgil and Spenser. There a human agent, Aeneas or Guyon, gazed in wonder as he approached a cluster of demonic personifications. Here the approaching figure is the demon, and the personifications suffer the fatal consequence of gazing at her. Her power exceeds that of the questing heroes she replaces, and her approach, obliterating the threshold between the realms of light and darkness, amounts to a wildly inverted Harrowing of Hell.

Still another revision of the traditional model appears in Gray's "Ode on a Distant Prospect of Eton College" (composed in 1742), where the threshold between worlds is replaced by the temporal boundary between present and future.[31] The poet, contemplating the doomed innocence of the schoolboys, sees a vision of "black Misfortune's baleful train," a "murtherous band" of passions and infirmities who wait to ambush the children as they descend into the "vale of years" (57, 59, 81).[32]

In each of these examples, a cluster of personifications has been stationed at a crucial threshold between opposing realms or conditions, and each is engaged, actually or potentially, in a violent or threatening confrontation. Each offers to block the progress of a questing or conquering agent; even Gray's innocents are involved, however unconsciously, in a perilous journey with symbolic affinities to an epic or romantic quest. Yet, in every case except Gray's ode, the abstractions turn out to be ineffectual opponents, easily avoided or conquered by the agents they confront. Despite their resemblance to the monsters of archaic ritual and myth, their role is not so much to enforce a boundary as to saturate it with explicit meaning. Except in *Paradise Lost,* the thresholds are in fact overcrowded with figures, while the figures in each group are so thematically consistent as to seem redundant. An effect of exhaustive signification, of thorough legibility, temporarily suspends the drama of heroic trespass. Such episodes provide a strangely extroverted alternative to the standard model of sublime self-consciousness: instead of a subject receiving a magnified sense of self in return for an experience of failure or terror, a narrative pauses long enough to allow the display of an abstract, public consciousness—a consciousness that need not be imputed to the agent whose journey has been temporarily halted.

If these passages from earlier works establish the traditional provenance of Wordsworth's tableau in "Yew-Trees," they also reveal its uniqueness. The number of personifications has been reduced, though not for the sake of ominous concentration, as in Milton's two formidable shapes. Heroic narrative survives only in the poem's allusions to ancient battles (Azincour, Crecy, and Poictiers), and even these disappear after the eighth line. The only vestiges of the sublime confrontation between an intruder and a throng of guardians are the disembodied "looks / that threaten the profane." There is, in fact, no longer any threshold to guard; the traditional gateway between two radically separate spaces has been rounded off into an opaque enclosure, with nothing of interest lying before or beyond it.[33] Wordsworth's placement of his abstractions inside the enclosure, "beneath [its] sable roof," further deprives them of their status as guardians.

They also lose their role as heraldic bearers of explicit meaning. As united worshippers or reposing listeners, they seem to have been relieved, for the moment, of their particular allegorical duties. Evil personifications make obvious sense at the gates of Hell, but the thematic relation of Wordsworth's figures to the Borrowdale grove—the "natural temple" of an unspecified faith—is at most implicit. Fear, trembling Hope, Silence, and the rest are no doubt appropriate, in a general sense, to the grove's funereal solemnity, and this appropriateness can be specified in various ways. Riffaterre, for example, after pages of detailed argument, refers the whole concluding passage to a single thematic "matrix": "We can rewrite lines 26–33 thus: *the sound of running water is enough to assuage Man's misery.*" On one level, this seems fair enough; the personifications indeed derive from "obsessive components of the human psyche," and can thus be taken as a fragmented image of "Man."[34] But nothing in the poem directly encourages us to reconstitute these figures as the thematic entity (human psyche) from which they derive. Nor is the grove itself, "a natural temple scattered o'er / With altars undisturbed of mossy stone," really ominous enough to provide a convincing setting for representations of human "misery." If these figures normally stand for misery, they seem to have abandoned their usual meanings before arriving at the grove.

Comparison with Wordsworth's sources, then, raises the question of whether his personifications in "Yew-Trees" are meant to function allegorically at all. Detached from their narrative and thematic roles, these figures primarily serve to fill an enclosure with abstract agents, agents that are neither human, like the poet or reader, nor monstrous, like the Furies in Collins' "baleful Grove" ("Ode to Fear," 37). Personifications on vacation from allegory, these casual worshippers neither frighten one away from their sacred enclosure nor invite one to join them. They neither challenge nor assuage our sense of our own agency, but simply shrug it off.

Read in this way, Wordsworth's "return" to formal personification remains consistent both with his characteristic attenuation of allegory and with his abstract and impersonal treatment of the sublime. "Yew-Trees," like "Resolution and Independence," exhibits a version of the sublime detached from the human interests imbedded in traditional structures of confrontation and ambivalence. The sublime, as we have encountered it in Collins, Burke, Kant, and Coleridge, was designed to put the self in touch with a source of archaic power without subjecting it to the fanaticism or bathos of total identification. And there is a strong temptation to read this poem—indeed, much of Wordsworth—as a softened or implicit version of the same ambivalent structure. But ambivalence in "Yew-Trees," as we have seen, reduces to something closer to indifference, an attitude after all appropriate to the alien longevity of the yews. Occupied by figures who are neither our enemies nor our surrogates, the Borrowdale grove is a space that neither excludes nor includes us: remarkably like the space of someone else's poem.

Propertie was thus appalled,
That the selfe was not the same . . .

> Shakespeare, "The Phoenix
> and the Turtle"

Epilogue:
Literal and Figurative Agency
in *Paradise Lost*

Raphael and the Phoenix

The archangel Raphael, on his way to warn Adam of Satan's plot, looks toward his destination from the gate of Heaven (*PL,* V.257–261):

> From hence, no cloud, or, to obstruct his sight,
> Star interpos'd, however small he sees,
> Not unconform to other shining Globes,
> Earth and the Gard'n of God, with Cedars crown'd
> Above all Hills.

The moment occasions a typical, though by Miltonic standards rather modest, simile, comparing the gazing angel first to an astronomer, then to a pilot (261–266):

> As when by night the Glass
> Of *Galileo,* less assur'd, observes
> Imagin'd Lands and Regions in the Moon:
> Or Pilot from amidst the *Cyclades*

Delos or *Samos* first appearing kens
A cloudy spot.

Immediately after this simile, Milton provides the following description of Raphael's descent to earth (266–274):

> Down thither prone in flight
> He speeds, and through the vast Ethereal Sky
> Sails between worlds and worlds, with steady wing
> Now on the polar winds, then with quick Fan
> Winnows the buxom Air; till within soar
> Of Tow'ring Eagles, to all the Fowls he seems
> A *Phoenix,* gaz'd by all, as that sole Bird
> When to enshrine his reliques in the Sun's
> Bright Temple, to *Egyptian Thebes* he flies.

Everything in the context and the construction of this passage encourages us to read the last three and a half lines as yet another simile, this one comparing Raphael's appearance, as it strikes the astonished fowls, to the impression a phoenix would make on human spectators. But this perfectly sensible reading is overturned by what happens when the angel lands (275–277, emphasis added):

> At once on th' Eastern cliff of Paradise
> He lights, *and to his proper shape returns*
> A Seraph wing'd . . .

The switch is stunning: what looked like a simile turns out to have been a literal transformation. Raphael, we now realize, had assumed a disguise, which he now abandons. Such a reading was possible all along; in the Renaissance, to "seem" a phoenix could mean to "counterfeit" one. But why should Raphael have concealed his proper shape? To protect the birds from being dazzled by his radiance? He takes no such precaution when approaching Adam and Eve—or the other animals, some of whom presumably see him in the garden. Thematically the disguise seems equally pointless. Scholars have suggested various iconographic reasons for *comparing* Raphael to the phoenix, a symbol of immortality, constancy, true love, and friendship; but iconography would be served just as well by a simile as by a literal metamorphosis.[1] The proximity of the Galileo simile, together with the absence of any motive for a literal disguise, irresistibly suggests that the likening of Raphael to a phoenix began as a figure of speech and then *turned literal.*

The reason for the switch remains obscure; perhaps Milton simply wanted a dramatic way of introducing his depiction of the angel's proper shape, which is now described for the first time (277–285). But the lack of a compelling reason is exactly the point. For it reveals the extremely low degree of Milton's commitment to a consistent separation of literal and figurative representations. This minor episode demonstrates on a small scale the tendency that bothered eighteenth-century critics when it took the more obvious form of mixing literal and figurative agents—confronting a "historical" being, Satan, with "fictitious" persons, Sin and Death. But Raphael's transformation is, in a way, the more telling case: precisely because it is such a minor, even casual occurrence, it testifies to the pervasiveness of the shift in attitudes that separates Milton from the eighteenth century—indeed, from virtually all post-Renaissance accounts of the relation between literal and figurative language. At the very least, it casts doubt on the assumption, common to eighteenth- and many twentieth-century readers, that the violation of realism in the episodes of Sin and Death is an exception to Milton's normal practice and demands a special justification. And to challenge that assumption is to raise a question implicit in much of the foregoing argument: does Milton share the interest in figurative agency that underlies subsequent notions of personification and the sublime?

Sin and Death in *Paradise Lost*

Since B. Rajan's observation, in 1947, that "with Satan, Sin and Death make a kind of infernal Trinity," complementing "its heavenly counterpart,"[2] more than a dozen critics have explored the structural and rhetorical felicities of Milton's allegory. A long succession of scholarly articles has traced its iconography to an equally long list of possible sources. These materials together amount to a virtually exhaustive commentary, which the present remarks will not attempt to assimilate or expand. My purpose in returning to the allegory is merely to raise, once again, the question of its relation to the rest of the poem—this time with the aim of deciding whether anything in Milton's intention corresponds to the eighteenth-century and Romantic thematizations of personification as such.

For the eighteenth-century critics discussed in Chapter 2, an interest in the difference between figurative and literal agency took the form of an uneasiness about Milton's insertion of allegory into the realistic space of the epic. Twentieth-century critics have defended the allegory in ways that nevertheless tend to reflect the same uneasiness evinced by Addison and his followers. The most ingenious modern defense is the one that treats Sin and Death as figments of Satan's (or the Satanic) imagination. The stiff unreality of allegory, according to this defense, is appropriate to the obsessive delusions of "fallen" consciousness. In an intriguing critical version of Miltonic theodicy, responsibility for the violation of realism is neatly shifted from Milton to Satan, just as responsibility for creating evil is shifted from God to Satan, Adam, and Eve. Anne Davidson Ferry, in a passage clearly indebted to Coleridge's strictures on allegory in general, provides the most explicit statement of the view that Sin and Death are symptoms of a mode of thinking distinct from the poet's own:

> The one sustained allegorical episode in the epic is used to illustrate the origin and effects of Satan's Fall. It is also a representation of the nature of his vision and the quality of his experience, for although the story has to be told to Satan, as well as to the reader, it originated actually within his own mind, springing from his head with the figure of Sin. In introducing us to Sin and Death, the narrator is forced to use a mode of language different from that which expresses his own unified vision because he is describing the creatures of Satan's disordered imagination. These creatures do exist but they exist *as personified abstractions* and not as divinely created unified beings . . . The very fact that Satan does not recognize his offspring and has forgotten the act of her creation is a further illustration of his divided consciousness. This discrepancy between his inner and outer experience is expressed in the form

of allegory, because the tendency which characterizes is fallen vision to disjoin physical and spiritual truths has its parallel in the allegorical method, which depends on the separation of concrete and abstract meanings.[3]

If accepted, Ferry's interpretation would bring the present argument to a perfect close: Milton, using allegory at once to embody fanatic agency and to reveal its unreality, would become the fullest practitioner of sublime personification. But Ferry's relegation of allegory to Satan's "fallen vision" requires the suppression of at least one uncomfortable detail. In book X, Sin and Death, on their way to earth after their parent's victory, are seen for the first time by an agent other than Satan. The agent is God the Father, whose infallible vision can hardly be subject to the delusional products of a fallen imagination. He not only sees them but takes their agency quite literally, to the point of responding rather testily to their mockery of his policies (616–626):

> See with what heat these Dogs of Hell advance
> To waste and havoc yonder World, which I
> So fair and good created, and had still
> Kept in that state, had not the folly of Man
> Let in these wasteful Furies, who impute
> Folly to mee, so doth the Prince of Hell
> And his Adherents, that with so much ease
> I suffer them to enter and possess
> A place so heav'nly, and conniving seem
> To gratify my scornful Enemies,
> That laugh . . .

This episode, together with the presence of allegorical figures in God's own speeches (for example, III.209–210: "He with his whole posterity must die, / Die hee or Justice must"), makes the distinction between divine and demonic modes of representation hard to sustain.

Some critics have in fact wanted to deny that the ontological status of Sin and Death can be distinguished at all sharply from that of the poem's literal agents. William Empson argues that "Milton regarded the words Sin and Death, in the poem, as the names of two supernatural persons, and wanted us to gather that the abstract ideas were named later from the predominant activites of those persons. With part of his mind, he claims to be inspired and able to tell us what really did happen."[4] Philip J. Gallagher drops Empson's qualifications—"in the poem"; "With part of his mind"—and asserts "that Sin and her son Death are consistently real (i.e., physical and historical) throughout Milton's major epic, their allegorical onomastics notwithstanding." Milton, according to Gallagher, "understands both his epics to be inspired elaborations of events (like the birth of Sin) many of which are only hinted at in the Scriptures." Moreover, "The insistent physicality of these individuals pressures the reader to regard their generation as a literal fact of cosmic history."[5] Gallagher does not deny that Sin and Death are made to carry allegorical meanings; on the contrary, Milton "clothes the real children of Satan in allegorical vesture."[6] But their essential historicity means that their presence in the poem in no way disrupts its ontological consistency.

This radical thesis is open to various objections. First, Milton's insistence, throughout his prose, on the adequacy of Scripture makes it seem unlikely that his references to poetic inspiration entail a claim that he has access to previously unrevealed historical facts. Second, if an agent like Sin is simultaneously real and allegorical, how do we determine where allegory ends and literal agency begins? And third, Sin's "physical" nature—half woman, half serpent—plainly derives from Spenser's monster Errour, which no one takes literally. The physicality of both Sin and Death, however "insistent" it may be, is allegorically conventional, as well as inconsistent in its details with the physical properties of the poem's other supernatural agents. The mode of Sin's birth, her pregnancy, the mere fact of her gender—all are anomalous departures from angelic biology, though easily explained in allegorical terms.[7]

Despite these difficulties, no argument can rule out the possibility that Empson's and Gallagher's, or Ferry's, account is correct. Once we grant that the inclusion of apparently figurative agents in an epic needs explaining, each of these explanations acquires a degree of plausibility. But our discussion of Raphael's metamorphosis raises the blander, if initially more

shocking, possibility that Milton was simply indifferent to the
mixing of literal and figurative agency, and therefore that Ferry's
separation and Gallagher's identification of allegory and realism are equally beside the point. This suspicion is confirmed
by a closer look at the self-presentation of Sin, whose ontology turns out to be too inconsistent to fit either of these
accounts.

Like Eve in book IV and Adam in book VIII, Sin in book
II (747–809) tells the story of her own origin. She recounts
her birth from the left side of Satan's head; the horrified reaction
of the rebellious angels, until her "attractive graces won / The
most averse"; her incestuous romance with an impregnation by
Satan, who viewed in her his "perfect image"; and the War in
Heaven, resulting in the expulsion of the rebels, including herself. During or after her fall (the syntax is unclear), the key to
the Gates of Hell "was giv'n" into her hand (she neglects to say
by whom).

Up to this point, her narrative is a transparent allegory: the
Athena-like parthenogenesis stands for the spontaneous origin
of pride in Satan and every subsequent sinner; Sin's seduction
of those she initially shocks indicates the gradual erosion of a
sinner's conscience by the force of habit; Sin holds the key to
Hell because sin is the cause of damnation. The fact that Satan
sees himself in Sin obviously supports the many critics who
have read the episode as a demonic parody of the Father's
generation of his perfect image, the Son. And the style of the
narrative is appropriate to allegory: setting and causality are
vague and arbitrary (where in Heaven do Sin and Satan hold
their trysts, why does she land at the outskirts of Hell instead
of on the burning lake, who exactly gives her the key and
when?). Together, these allegorical features distinguish Sin's
narrative from every previous episode in the poem, and Sin
herself from every previous agent.[8]

The next turn in her narrative, however, is difficult to assimilate to conventional notions of allegorical personality. We left
her holding the key at the Gates of Hell; here is the rest of her
narrative (777–809):

> Pensive here I sat
> Alone, but long I sat not, till my womb
> Pregnant by thee, and now excessive grown
> Prodigious motion felt and rueful throes.
> At last this odious offspring whom thou seest
> Thine own begotten, breaking violent way
> Tore through my entrails, that with fear and pain
> Distorted, all my nether shape thus grew
> Transform'd: but he my inbred enemy
> Forth issu'd, brandishing his fatal Dart
> Made to destroy: I fled, and cri'd out *Death;*
> Hell trembl'd at the hideous Name, and sigh'd
> From all her Caves, and back resounded *Death.*
> I fled, but he pursu'd (though more, it seems,
> Inflam'd with lust than rage) and swifter far,
> Mee overtook his mother all dismay'd,
> And in embraces forcible and foul
> Ingend'ring with me, of that rape begot
> These yelling Monsters that with ceaseless cry
> Surround me, as thou saw'st, hourly conceiv'd
> And hourly born, with sorrow infinite
> To me, for when they list, into the womb
> That bred them they return, and howl and gnaw
> My Bowels, thir repast; then bursting forth
> Afresh with conscious terrors vex me round,
> That rest or intermission none I find.
> Before mine eyes in opposition sits
> Grim *Death* my Son and foe, who sets them on,
> And me his Parent would full soon devour
> For want of other prey, but that he knows
> His end with mine involv'd; and knows that I
> Should prove a bitter Morsel, and his bane,
> Whenever that shall be; so Fate pronounc'd.

Joseph H. Summers is surely right to see comedy here "in the distance between the ceremonious tone and the appalling content": "The violences of her labour and of her attitude toward her son are too much for utter suavity, yet her assumption of the correctness of her responses and the injustice of her misfortunes never wavers."[9] The peculiar discrepancy between tone and content works simultaneously against allegory *and* realism. Sin's evident distaste for the whole affair coexists with an almost urbane detachment, even with what looks strangely like irony at her own expense: what else do we make of the parenthetical reflection that Death was "more, it seems, / Inflam'd wth lust than rage"? If her detachment prevents a realistic interpretation of her agony, it also keeps her from seeming appropriately absorbed in the Satanic evil she ostensibly personifies. But the oddest detail in this passage, the one most difficult to reconcile with continuous allegory, appears in the first sentence.

> Pensive here I sat
> Alone, but long I sat not, till my womb
> Pregnant by thee, and now excessive grown
> Prodigious motion felt and rueful throes.

Pensive: but what can Sin have been thinking about? Brief as it is, her moment of speculative leisure endows her with an empirical consciousness wholly inexplicable in allegorical terms. It ancitipates, in fact, the representation of Eve's consciousness in the moment of her first awakening: "much wond'ring where / And what I was, whence thither brought, and how" (IV.451–452). And the posture of pensive sitting recurs explicitly in Adam's autobiography in book VIII: "On a green shady Bank profuse of Flow'rs / Pensive I sat me down . . . (286–287).

These parallels cannot mean, I think, that Milton intends an ironic connection among the three cases of pensiveness, even though the episodes are thematically related in other respects. Pensiveness must simply strike him as appropriate to a newly created consciousness with little to remember and nothing to do. But precisely the fact that she has nothing to do but think— aimlessly, wistfully?—displaces Sin from the thematic role that, in proper allegory, should define her agency at every moment. As the personification of Satan's rebellious pride, she ought to spend her free time plotting, preening, or lusting for Satan. Instead, at least until her pregnancy overtakes her, she seems to have been relieved of her allegorical duties, not unlike the quiet personifications of Wordsworth's "Yew-Trees."

Her vacation, of course, is abruptly canceled, and allegory

returns with the "conscious terrors" that vex [her] round" as
they would any sinner, as well as with her theologically motivated announcment that Death knows his demise will be linked
with hers. After Sin's speech, Satan unhesitatingly forges an
alliance with the shapes he earlier found strange and "detesta-
ble" (745). His utter lack of surprise at Sin's narrative, which
conflicts with everyone else's recollection of the angels' rebellion and fall, indicates that he too has been displaced, temporarily, from his ordinary status, and has been reduced to an
equivalence with allegorical agents who otherwise would have
continued to appall him. Sin's sudden acquisition of a more than
allegorical consciousness, together with Satan's sudden loss of
it, suggests that historical and allegorical agency are readily in-
terchangeable—even in the career of a single agent—and that
Milton has no consistent interest either in separating or reconciling the two.

Nor is this the indifference deliberately sought by Wordsworth, in a poem like "Yew-Trees," as an attenuated expression
of sublime ambivalence (see Chapter 4). If Wordsworth in one
sense returns to Milton, he nevertheless stands at the opposite
end of the century in which figurative language acquired a thematic interest that virtually any later attitude toward poetry was
bound to reflect.

Milton and the Coleridgean Interest in Literature

The conclusion reached in the foregoing section—that Milton
was merely indifferent to the oscillation between literal and
figurative agency that scandalized his eighteenth-century critics—applies to Milton's poetry, not his prose. Outside poetry,
Milton shared the suspicion of figurative language common to
Puritan theologians and proponents of the new empirical science.[10] He allowed the mixing of allegorical and historical agency
in a poem, perhaps because of the precedent of Spenser, perhaps
for the sorts of theoretical reasons advanced in Mazzoni's *Defense of Dante* or in the *Theatrum Poetarum* of his own nephew
and pupil Edward Phillips.[11] There is no need, according to this
view, to explain Milton's allegorical practice by considering him

the last embodiment of an antediluvian consciousness that somehow washed up on the shores of the Enlightenment. If Milton
distinguished sharply between poetic fiction and ordinary belief,
what sets him apart from his eighteenth-century and Romantic
successors is his lack of a thematic interest in the distinction.

Milton seems to have lacked, in other words, what might be
called the Coleridgean interest in literature. A broader argument might establish what the present one can only suggest:
that the interest in sublime personification that runs through
English letters from Addison to Coleridge is only the most
abstract expression of an ambivalence at the heart of the post-
Renaissance interest in literary fiction as such. The ambivalence
consists in a desire to possess the power of alien or archaic
belief while at the same time avoiding its absurd or violent
consequences. The ideal solution to such ambivalence is embodied in the Coleridgean conception of literature as a reconciling medium between fiction and literal belief. But I suggest,
at the risk of sounding too readily teleological, that the ideal
was implicit throughout the eighteenth century in notions of
literature not simply as a mixture of pleasure and instruction
but as a form of epistemological leisure: a way, that is, of holding
beliefs one knows to be false—or can't admit one holds.[12]

Any broader account of these developments will necessarily
trace them to a variety of overlapping causes. But in the most
general terms (the account might run), the eighteenth-century
desire to moderate the attraction of powerful representations
with an insistence on their fictionality seems to have derived
from the propitious conjunction of a political reality and a philosophical anomaly. The political reality included the liberal reaction—still prominent in Coleridge—to seventeenth-century
religious violence. The philosophical anomaly lay in an increasingly rigid distinction between empirical perception and other
forms of representation. This distinction was in turn conflated
with the (logically unrelated) distinctions between literal and
figurative utterances, and between truth and poetic fiction. Beliefs themselves were increasingly viewed as bits of conscious
representaton detached from the world of perceptual fact.[13] Like
other fictional products, beliefs could be imagined or "enter-
tained" by an urbanely uncommitted mind. Conversely, imag-

inative writers came to be viewed, half-seriously, as hallucinating enthusiasts who mistook their own opinions for perceptual facts.

No doubt a central figure here is Locke, in whom the political reaction against religious violence and the epistemology of "literal" perception so authoritatively converged. It was Addison's genius to propose the pleasures of literary fiction (including personification) as a means of experimenting with non-empirical modes of belief at a safe remove.[14] And, the broader account might conclude, the grounds of this general post-Renaissance interest in literature as a mode of epistemological leisure have never essentially shifted, despite a series of displacements in specific literary practices and concerns.

Literature, conceived as epistemological leisure, is a means of both isolating and preserving alien, dangerous, or ludicrous beliefs. In theorists from Addison to Coleridge to I. A. Richards, it becomes a form of epistemological toleration, parallel to the religious toleration that had its origins in the same political and intellectual milieu. The function of detaching beliefs from the consequences of believing is never, in fact, a strictly literary affair. As the examples of Coleridge and Kant suggest, the notion of literature as a repository of fictionalized beliefs finds a close analogue in broader philosophical and political attempts to imagine the *self* as a medium between private illusions and normative truth. And the analogy works both ways. Not only has literature served as a means of collecting eccentric, fanatic, or otherwise specialized selves; since the Renaissance, literary works have in turn been subjected to constant allegorization as ideal images of the self—the self, that is, as liberal thought has wanted to conceive it.[15]

The present brief history has had a narrower, though related, subject. It has concentrated on a highly specialized class of fictional "selves," personified abstractions. To a poet like Milton, these agents possessed no intrinsic philosophical interest; they counted as impressive and instructive additions to a frankly spectacular and didactic poem. But in later writers these already allegorical agents were enlisted in a further allegory: with their peculiar combination of power and fictionality, they came to personify an emerging political and philosophical ideal of literary agency itself.

Abbreviations

PE   Edmund Burke, *A Philosophical Enquiry into the Origin of
        Our Ideas of the Sublime and Beautiful,* ed. James T. Boulton.
        Notre Dame: Notre Dame University Press, 1968.

PL   *Paradise Lost,* in *John Milton: Complete Poems and Major Prose,*
        ed. Meritt Y. Hughes, pp. 176–469. New York: Odyssey,
        1957.

PrW   *The Prose Works of William Wordsworth,* ed. W. J. B. Owen
        and Jane Worthington Smyser, 3 vols. Oxford: Clarendon,
        1974.

PWC   *The Complete Poetical Works of Samuel Taylor Coleridge,* ed. Er-
        nest Hartley Coleridge, 2 vols. Oxford: Clarendon, 1912.

PWW   *The Poetical Works of William Wordsworth,* ed. Ernest de Se-
        lincourt and Helen Darbishire, 5 vols. Oxford: Clarendon,
        1940–1949.

Notes

Introduction

1. M. H. Abrams, "Wordsworth and Coleridge on Diction and Figures," in *English Institute Essays, 1952,* ed. *Alan S. Downer* (1954; rpt. New York: AMS Press, 1965), pp. 171–201.

2. My treatment of the relations between "Enlightened" poetics and pre-Enlightenment or "Gothic" agency is indebted in various ways to the writings of Geoffrey H. Hartman, especially to the essays on the subject collected in *Beyond Formalism: Literary Essays, 1958–1970* (New Haven: Yale University Press, 1970) and *The Fate of Reading and Other Essays* (Chicago: University of Chicago Press, 1975).

3. Henry Home (Lord Kames), *Elements of Criticism,* 6th ed. (1785; rpt. in facsimile New York: Garland, 1972), II, 394. Kames is stating a general principle that he does not, however, apply to Milton's allegory.

4. On the role of urbane detachment even in the most declamatory eighteenth-century poetry, see Marshall Brown, "The Urbane Sublime," *ELH,* 45 (1978), 236–254.

5. *The Stateman's Manual,* in *LS,* p. 30.

6. On personification in Thomson, see Ralph Cohen, *The Unfolding of "The Seasons"* (London: Routledge and Kegan Paul, 1970), esp. pp. 24–27. For Johnson's "rhetorical" (as opposed to allegorical or descriptive) use of

personification, see Donald Davie, *Purity of Diction in English Verse* (New York: Oxford University Press, 1953), pp. 38–47; and Chester F. Chapin, *Personification in Eighteenth-Century English Poetry* (1954; rpt. New York: Octagon, 1974), chap. 6.

7. Northrop Frye, *Fearful Symmetry: A Study of William Blake* (Princeton: Princeton University Press, 1947), p. 117.

1. Coleridge on Allegory and Violence

1. John Payne Collier, *Seven Lectures on Shakespeare and Milton by the Late S. T. Coleridge* (London, 1856), p. 64.

2. Both arguments are ultimately Aristotelian; see *Poetics,* chap. 25, in *The Basic Writings of Aristotle,* ed. Richard McKeon (New York: Random House, 1941), pp. 1483–1484.

3. *Romeo and Juliet,* I.i.178–184; Collier's punctuation.

4. Collier, *Seven Lectures,* pp. 64–66. For a brief remark anticipating this association of Milton's description with the instability of perception, see *The Notebooks of Samuel Taylor Coleridge,* ed. Kathleen Coburn, II (Princeton: Princeton University Press, 1973), 3256.

Joseph Anthony Wittreich, Jr., who includes this excerpt from Collier's book in his very useful collection of Romantic comments on Milton, suggests that Blake is the "only exception to Coleridge's observation" on the failure of painters to respect Milton's obscurity. In fact, however, in Blake's versions Death is transparent but nevertheless distinctly outlined, in accordance with Blake's well-known aesthetic. Besides Blake, distinguished illustrators of the episode included Fuseli, Hogarth, and James Gillray. For Wittreich's account, see *The Romantics on Milton: Formal Essays and Critical Asides* (Cleveland: Press of Case Western Reserve University, 1970), p. 286n77; see also his *Angel of Apocalypse: Blake's Idea of Milton* (Madison: University of Wisconsin Press, 1975), pp. 94–95, 287n40. For a full discussion of the importance of Milton's allegory in English painting of the later eighteenth century, see Ronald Paulson, *Book and Painting: Shakespeare, Milton and the Bible: Literary Texts and the Emergence of English Painting* (Knoxville: University of Tennessee Press, 1982), pp. 104–115.

5. *PE,* pp. 58–64. Coleridge later disparaged Burke's treatise: "Burke's Essay on the Sublime and Beautiful seems to me a poor thing; and what he says upon Taste is neither profound nor accurate" (*Table Talk,* July 12, 1827, in *CWC,* VI, 293).

6. Coleridge's views on the sublime are difficult to sort out. Raimonda Modiano has recently argued that Coleridge rejected the "negative" features of the sublime (such as terror, privation, and failure of comprehension) shared by the theories of Burke and Kant ("Coleridge and the Sublime: A Response to Thomas Weiskel's *The Romantic Sublime," Wordsworth Circle,* 9, 1978, 110–120). Instead, according to Modiano, Coleridge favored a notion of the sublime as a "natural" and continuous "ascent" of the mind "into the realm of

ideas," without the need of a "stimulus from the defeat of the imagination": "his form of transcendence occurs gradually, not violently, through an intense engagement with the objects of sense, and not through an abrupt disconnection from them" (p. 117). Similarly, Elinor S. Shaffer claims that Coleridge collapsed the distinction between sublime and beautiful "by absorbing the beautiful into the sublime" and calling the resultant single category "the beautiful" ("Coleridge's Revolution in the Standard of Taste," *Journal of Aesthetics and Art Criticism,* 28, 1969, 213–221). Both arguments depend on complex inferences from Coleridge's German sources, incidental comments, and shifting terminology. Fortunately, there is no need here to establish a Coleridgean theory of the sublime; I use the term at this point merely to indicate a set of related issues. But there can be no doubt that, in the quoted paragraph, Coleridge is working directly in the tradition of Burke.

7. For a recent survey of Coleridge's attitudes, see John Gatta, Jr., "Coleridge and Allegory," *Modern Language Quarterly,* 38 (1977), 62–77. Gatta's thesis is that Coleridge's dislike for allegory has been exaggerated by critics who have overlooked his admiration for Dante, Spenser, and Bunyan: "What the record finally reveals . . . is an intriguing combination of ambivalence and ambiguity in Coleridge's critical attitude toward allegory" (p. 77).

8. Critics usually treat Coleridge's views on allegory, as I do, in connection with his opposing notion of the "symbol." Commentaries, from a wide range of viewpoints, include René Wellek, *A History of Modern Criticism, 1750–1950,* II (New Haven: Yale University Press, 1955), 174–175; Angus Fletcher, *Allegory: The Theory of a Symbolic Mode* (Ithaca: Cornell University Press, 1964), pp. 15–19; Patricia A. Ward, "Coleridge's Critical Theory of the Symbol," *Texas Studies in Literature and Language,* 8 (1966–1967), 27–32; Paul de Man, "The Rhetoric of Temporality," in *Interpretation: Theory and Practice,* ed. Charles S. Singleton (Baltimore: Johns Hopkins University Press, 1969), pp. 176–178; Mary Rahme, "Coleridge's Concept of Symbolism," *Studies in English Literature, 1500–1900,* 9 (1969), 620–622; Douglas Brownlow Wilson, "Two Modes of Apprehending Nature: A Gloss on the Coleridgean Symbol," *PMLA,* 87 (1972), 46–48; James D. Boulger, "Coleridge on Imagination Revisited," *Wordsworth Circle,* 4 (1973), 15–16; M. H. Abrams, "Coleridge and the Romantic Vision of the World," in *Coleridge's Variety: Bicentenary Studies,* ed. John Beer (London: Macmillan, 1974), pp. 130–131; Jonathan Culler, "Literary History, Allegory, and Semiology," *New Literary History,* 7 (1975–1976), 262–264, 269n4; J. Robert Barth, S.J., *The Symbolic Imagination: Coleridge and the Romantic Tradition* (Princeton: Princeton University Press, 1978); Jerome C. Christensen, "The Symbol's Errant Allegory: Coleridge and His Critics," *ELH,* 45 (1978), 640–659; Frances Ferguson, "Coleridge on Language and Delusion," *Genre,* 2 (1978), 196–197; John A. Hodgson, "Transcendental Tropes: Coleridge's Rhetoric of Allegory and Symbol," in *Allegory, Myth, and Symbol,* ed. Morton W. Bloomfield (Cambridge, Mass.: Harvard University Press, 1981), pp. 273–292; Thomas McFarland, *Romanticism and the Forms of Ruin: Wordsworth, Coleridge, and*

Modalities of Fragmentation (Princeton: Princeton University Press, 1981), 31–34; Leslie Brisman, "Coleridge and the Supernatural," *Studies in Romanticism,* 21 (1982), 123–159.

9. *MC,* p. 30. A condensed but also somewhat jumbled version of the definition is repeated in notes to a lecture on Spenser (pp. 32–33).

10. Coleridge's account of the relation between allegory and polytheism is echoed by C. S. Lewis' remark that "the twilight of the gods is the mid-morning of the personifications" (*The Allegory of Love: A Study in Medieval Tradition,* London: Oxford University Press, 1936, p. 52). Lewis' entire discussion of late classical allegory (pp. 48–83) reads like a sympathetic elaboration of Coleridge's condensed history, though Coleridge is not mentioned; and in fact Lewis draws heavily on the Coleridgean philosopher Owen Barfield.

11. Cf. Gatta, "Coleridge and Allegory," p. 69: "At any time the uneasy marriage between allegorical tenor and vehicle could dissolve, just as the delicate balance between an allegorical agent's individual personhood and personified meaning could easily be lost."

12. *Coleridge on the Seventeenth Century,* ed. Roberta Florence Brinkley (Durham: Duke University Press, 1955), p. 575.

13. *The Stateman's Manual,* in *LS,* pp. 28–29.

14. The choice depends on context and not, apparently, on chronology. A version of the same distinction between allegory and symbol appears in notes for an 1818 lecture on Cervantes (*MC,* p. 99). This later version does shift the emphasis somewhat from the mode of figurative relation to the degrees of *deliberateness* in each case: allegory "cannot be other than spoken consciously," but in the symbol, "it is very possible that the general truth may be working unconsciously in the writer's mind." But this new point is not developed.

15. De Man, "Rhetoric of Temporality," pp. 177–178; Culler, "Literary History," pp. 263–264; Ferguson, "Coleridge on Language," p. 197; Christensen, "Symbol's Errant Allegory"; Hodgson, "Transcendental Tropes."

16. Thus de Man: "Starting out from the assumed superiority of the symbol in terms of organic substantiality, we end up with a description of figurative language as translucence, a description in which the distinction between allegory and symbol has become of secondary importance" (pp. 177–178). Culler: "Despite Coleridge's categorical and . . . overdetermined preference for the symbolic, in its better moments literature exposes the difficulty of this synecdochic mode of discourse by trying to employ it" (p. 264). Ferguson: "the insubstantiality of allegorical unity becomes hard to separate from the insubstantiality of the symbolic 'consubstantial translucence' " (p. 197). And Christensen: "in Coleridge the . . . wish for a metaphysical continuity that is involved in his promotion of the symbol is typically breached by a discourse that divulges the obdurate discontinuities of signification" (p. 644). For the claim that the notion of "symbol," in Coleridge and others, amounts to a "defensive strategy" that tries to conceal the "authentically temporal predicament" of the self, see de Man, p. 191. Similarly, for Culler, Coleridge's

denigration of allegory is "a nice strategy for exorcizing any doubts about the power of the poetical spirit" (p. 263).

17. The reduction of Coleridge's symbol to an unremarkable figure of speech goes back at least to Wellek, who claims that "the examples of symbol would seem to be mere instances of synecdoche, a figure of contiguity from which symbol cannot even develop" (*History*, II, 174).

18. De Man, "Rhetoric of Temporality," p. 177.

19. *The Literary Remains of Samuel Taylor Coleridge*, ed. Henry Nelson Coleridge, in *CWC*, V, 224. For the symbolic status of marriage itself, see *Aids to Reflection*, in *CWC*, I, 138n. Earlier in the same work, but without explicitly using the term "symbol," Coleridge contrasts the formalism of the Law with the consubstantial relations between Christian ritual and the religion as a whole (*CWC*, I, 128). A more colorful version of the remark on the Eucharist is recorded in the *Table Talk* entry for May 20, 1830: "The errors of the Sacramentaries on the one hand, and of the Romanists on the other, are equally great. The first have volatilized the Eucharist into a metaphor; the last have condensed it into an idol" (*CWC*, VI, 316–317).

20. Readers of J. L. Austin will be struck by the "performative" character of Coleridge's example: like a performative utterance, the anniversary helps to effect the relation it announces. Austin's first example of a performative is in fact the sentence "I do"—"as uttered in the course of the marriage ceremony" (*How to Do Things with Words*, 2nd ed., ed. J. O. Urmson and Marina Sbisà, Cambridge, Mass.: Harvard University Press, 1975, p. 5).

21. This is not to deny that Coleridge's interest in the symbol is, on the whole, theologically motivated. For an eloquent insistence on the specifically Christian provenance of symbolic participation throughout Coleridge's writings, see Brisman, "Coleridge and the Supernatural."

22. Cf. Rahme, who points to the same puzzle but resolves it with reference to "the metaphysical basis of Coleridge's poetic theory" ("Coleridge's Concept of Symbolism," p. 622). For a subtle—and also highly critical—treatment of Coleridge on analogy, see Hodgson, "Transcendental Tropes," pp. 288–292.

23. For an excellent account of the issues surrounding the doctrine of accommodation, see H. R. MacCallum, "Milton and Figurative Interpretation of the Bible," *University of Toronto Quarterly*, 31 (1961–1962), 397–415.

24. On Coleridge's "coinage" of "tautegorical," see editor White's account, *LS*, p. 30n3.

25. Cf. the following remark in the Conclusion to *Aids to Reflection;* once again Coleridge is attacking Socinian empiricism: "Now I do not hesitate to assert, that it was one of the great purposes of Christianity . . . to rouse and emancipate the soul from this debasing slavery to the outward senses, to awaken the mind to the true *criteria* of reality, namely, permanence, power, will manifested in act, and truth operating as life." The Gospel recalled "the drowsed soul from the dreams and phantom world of sensuality to *actual* reality" (*CWC*, I, 363–364).

26. For a commentary on the entire passage and its relation to Coleridge's metascientific speculations, see Abrams, "Coleridge and the Romantic Vision," pp. 126–131. On the centrality of biological analogy in Coleridge's aesthetics, see M. H. Abrams, *The Mirror and the Lamp: Romantic Theory and the Critical Tradition* (New York: Oxford University Press, 1953), pp. 68–69, 167–177.

27. Samuel Taylor Coleridge to William Sotheby, September 10, 1802, *Collected Letters of Samuel Taylor Coleridge,* ed. Earl Leslie Griggs, 6 vols. (Oxford: Clarendon, 1956–1971), II, 864. The importance of Coleridge's relation to Bowles has been stressed in several commentaries. See for example M. H. Abrams, "Wordsworth and Coleridge on Diction and Figures," in *English Institute Essays, 1952,* ed. Alan S. Downer (1954; rpt. New York: AMS Press, 1965), pp. 194–196; W. K. Wimsatt, Jr., "The Structure of Romantic Nature Imagery," in *The Verbal Icon: Studies in the Meaning of Poetry* (Lexington: University Press of Kentucky, 1954), pp. 105–108; M. H. Abrams, "Structure and Style in the Greater Romantic Lyric," in *From Sensibility to Romanticism: Essays Presented to Frederick A. Pottle,* ed. Frederick W. Hilles and Harold Bloom (New York: Oxford University Press, 1965), pp. 539–544, 547–551.

28. Coleridge to Sotheby, September 10, 1802, *Collected Letters,* II, 865–866. The fact that Coleridge goes on in the same letter (pp. 866–867) to recommend an ingenious allegorical interpretation of a passage in Milton's *Comus* suggests that the explicit alignment of allegory and fancy is not yet in place.

29. Ibid., II, 864; emphasis on the last phrase added.

30. The editors note (*BL,* I, 30n4) that the "use of *Schwärmerei* for 'fanaticism' dates back at least as far as Luther (1527)." The importance of *Schwärmerei* as a polemical term in Kant is taken up in Chapter 3.

31. I refer to *Coleridge's* Hamlet; see *Coleridge's Shakespearean Criticism,* ed. Thomas Middleton Raysor (Cambridge, Mass.: Harvard University Press, 1930), I, 37.

32. Coleridge is slightly misquoting Dryden's *Absalom and Achitophel,* I.163–164. Dryden's couplet: "Great wits are sure to madness near allied, / And thin partitions do their bounds divide" (see *BL,* I, 44n3).

33. An explicit application of the adjectives "centripetal" and "centrifugal" to the issue of aesthetic balance appears in the adaptation of an oration by Schelling that Coleridge titles "On Poesy or Art" (1818): "In order to derive pleasure from the occupation of the mind, the principle of unity must always be present, so that in the midst of the multeity the centripetal force be never suspended, nor the sense be fatigued by the predominance of the centrifugal force" (*Biographia Literaria,* ed. John Shawcross, Oxford: Clarendon, 1907, II, 262). This *balancing* of "unity in multeity" Coleridge calls "the principle of beauty"—unlike the *oscillation* between them that constitutes the sublimity of Milton's Death.

34. See *Coleridge on the Seventeenth Century,* pp. 587–588, for an 1810 ms. version of the same remark. As editor Brinkley comments, "Few ideas

have been more often repeated by Coleridge than this famous comparison. It was given almost verbatim in the lectures on Milton and so impressed the reporters that they took it down with unusual accuracy for the newspapers" (p. 588n82).

35. Ibid., pp. 556–557.

36. *Table Talk,* May 12, 1830, in *CWC,* VI, 312–313.

37. *Table Talk,* August 18, 1833, in *CWC,* VI, 479.

38. The context of this well-known phrase is worth recalling. Coleridge is recounting his difficulties in accepting Trinitarian doctrine. He was especially bothered by the sacrificial violence of the atonement. He could accept the philosophical notion of the Logos "as *hypostasized* (i.e. neither a mere attribute or a personification)," but this doctrine "in no respect removed my doubts concerning the incarnation and the redemption by the cross; which I could neither reconcile *in reason* with the impassiveness of the Divine Being, nor in my moral feelings with the sacred distinction between things and persons, the vicarious payment of a debt and the vicarious expiation of guilt" (*BL,* I, 204–205). The solution awaited the "more thorough revolution in my philosophic principles" that it is the business of the *Biographia* to record.

39. *PWC,* II, 1097–1108. The probable date of the occasion and the names of the participants are supplied by editor Coleridge. For a brief but suggestive account of the preface in the context of a wider discussion of the relation between Coleridge's politics and his poetics, see Reeve Parker, *Coleridge's Meditative Art* (Ithaca: Cornell University Press, 1975), pp. 85–87.

40. The poem is too long to quote in full. But the last lines of Fire to her sisters (as printed in the poem's first version, in the *Morning Post,* January 8, 1798) give an adequate sample. Slaughter and Famine have just announced their plan to compensate Pitt for his services by stirring up a mob to "tear him limb from limb." Fire reproaches them with ingratitude (*PWC,* I, 239 app. crit.):

> [To *Slaughter.*
> For *you* he turn'd the dust to mud
> With his fellow creatures' blood!
> [To *Famine.*
> And hunger scorch'd as many more,
> To make *your* cup of joy run o'er.
> [To *Both.*
> Full ninety moons, he by my troth!
> Hath richly cater'd for you both!
> And in an hour would you repay
> An eight years' debt? Away! away!
> I alone am faithful! I
> Cling to him everlastingly.

The satirical target is not explicitly named in the poem, though each of the personifications reminds us that "Four letters form his name."

41. *The Friend,* ed. Barbara E. Rooke, 2 vols. (vol. 4 of *The Collected Works of Samuel Taylor Coleridge,* Princeton: Princeton University Press. 1969), I, 139; II, 116. The essay on Luther in which this remark appears was mainly a translation of an excerpt from a travel guide by Jonas Ludwig von Hess, but the decision to exclude the passage from Luther's address was Coleridge's; see Rooke's notes, I, 136, 139.

42. Smith, a Whig member of Parliament, had spoken against Southey in the House of Commons; see Erdman's notes, *EOT,* II, 450–451.

43. *Luther: Selected Political Writings,* various trans., ed. and introd. J. M. Porter (Philadelphia: Fortress, 1974), p. 86.

44. Ibid., pp. 91, 98.

45. *An Open Letter on the Harsh Book,* in *Luther: Selected Political Writings,* pp. 92–93. Cf. in the same volume the excerpt from *Temporal Authority: To What Extent It Should Be Obeyed* (1523), pp. 53–60. For a lucid critical explication of Luther's political doctrines, see Sheldon S. Wolin, *Politics and Vision: Continuity and Innovation in Western Political Thought* (Boston: Little, Brown, 1960), pp. 141–164. Luther's final position on the possibilities of Christian resistance to the state is ambiguous; see Porter's Introduction to *Luther: Selected Political Writings,* pp. 15–17.

46. *Luther: Selected Political Writings,* pp. 74–75, 93; cf. Porter's Introduction, pp. 12, 15, 19.

47. For explicit citations, see for example *Luther: Selected Political Writings,* pp. 25, 35, 56, 57, 75, 88, 95, 104, 105, 141.

48. Wolin, *Politics and Vision,* p. 145.

49. *The Friend,* I, 140; cf. II, 119.

50. *Table Talk,* July 25, 1832, in *CWC,* VI, 406.

51. *Inquiring Spirit: A New Presentation of Coleridge from His Published and Unpublished Prose Writings,* ed. Kathleen Coburn (London: Routledge and Kegan Paul, 1951), p. 149.

52. R. A. Knox, *Enthusiasm: A Chapter in the History of Religion* (Oxford: Clarendon, 1950), pp. 152–153. On the need to desynonymize enthusiasm and fanaticism, see *Inquiring Spirit,* pp. 102–103; cf. pp. 143, 397–398. Enthusiasm is a frequent topic of *Aids to Reflection;* see *CWC,* I, 153, 155–157, 199, 353–356. Coleridge discusses the fanaticism of the Peasants' War in *BL,* I, 197–198. In *The Friend,* he calls for a restoration of "true Christian *enthusiasm*" as the only way to "drive out the demons of fanaticism from the people" (I, 432).

53. Thomas McFarland, *Coleridge and the Pantheist Tradition* (Oxford: Clarendon, 1969), p. 107.

54. G. W. F. Hegel, *Early Theological Writings,* trans. T. M. Knox and Richard Kroner (1948; corr. ed. Philadelphia: University of Pennsylvania Press, 1971), p. 260.

55. *Table Talk,* December 18, 1831, in *CWC,* VI, 379.

56. *Coleridge on the Seventeenth Century,* p. 556.

57. Abrams, "Coleridge and the Romantic Vision," p. 110; for the full discussion of conversion, see pp. 104–115.

58. "Questions Concerning Certain Faculties Claimed for Man," in *Collected Papers of C. S. Peirce,* ed. Charles Hartshorne and Paul Weiss, V (Cambridge, Mass.: Harvard University Press, 1934), par. 235.

59. Peirce, "Questions Concerning Faculties," par. 233. The passage is discussed by Walter Benn Michaels in a fascinating account of Peirce's attack on Cartesian intuition in "The Interpreter's Self: Peirce on the Cartesian 'Subject,' " *Georgia Review,* 31 (1977), 392–394.

60. Erik H. Erikson, despite his role in popularizing a developmental interpretation of conversions, discusses the way a subject's resistance to commitment—through a "self-decreed moratorium" on choosing a career, for instance—contributes to the intensity of the conversion when it finally takes place; see his *Young Man Luther: A Study in Psychoanalysis and History* (New York: Norton, 1958), pp. 41–46.

61. Augustine, *The City of God,* trans. Henry Bettenson, ed. David Knowles (New York: Penguin, 1972), bk. XXII, chap. 30, p. 1089.

62. Ibid., bk. XI, chap. 12, p. 444.

63. *Coleridge's Shakespearean Criticism,* II, 204–205.

64. On the peculiar status of Coleridge's imaginary "correspondent," see Jerome C. Christensen, *Coleridge's Blessed Machine of Language* (Ithaca: Cornell University Press, 1981), pp. 169–175.

2. Milton's Allegory of Sin and Death in Eighteenth-Century Criticism

1. *PE,* p. 59. Since Burke misquotes it, I have taken Milton's passage from *PL,* p. 248.

2. Samuel H. Monk, *The Sublime: A Study of Critical Theories in XVIII-Century England* (New York: Modern Language Association, 1935), p. 20. See also pp. 22, 49, 56–57, 61, 68–69, and 103 for several of Monk's many references to Milton's reputation for sublimity. The chief responsibility for this commonplace belongs to Addison (Monk, *The Sublime,* pp. 56–57), though Milton's sublimity was already acknowledged by Dryden (pp. 43–44). For additional eighteenth-century comments, see chap. 1 of Raymond Dexter Havens' massive survey, *The Influence of Milton on English Poetry* (Cambridge, Mass.: Harvard University Press, 1922).

3. No. 309 of *The Spectator,* ed. Donald F. Bond, 5 vols. (Oxford: Clarendon, 1965), III, 120. Subsequent references to this edition will be given by number, volume, and page.

4. Francis Atterbury to Alexander Pope, November 8, 1717, *The Correspondence of Alexander Pope,* ed. George Sherburn (Oxford: Clarendon, 1956), I, 452. At the end of the century, Atterbury's remark was cited with approval

by William Cowper in his *Latin and Italian Poems of Milton Translated into English Verse, and a Fragment of a Commentary on Paradise Lost*, ed. William Hayley (London, 1808), p. 218; and by Thomas Green, *Extracts from the Diary of a Lover of Literature* (Ipswich, 1810), p. 192 (entry for February 2, 1800).

5. James Paterson, *A Complete Commentary, with Etymological, Explanatory, Critical and Classical Notes on Milton's Paradise Lost* (London, 1744), pp. 225, 249; Thomas Gibbons, *Rhetoric; or, A View of Its Principal Tropes and Figures* (1767; rpt. in facsimile Menston, England: Scholar Press, 1969), pp. 356–357.

6. Published in the *Spectator* each Saturday from January 5 to May 3, 1712. Addison's opinions are mentioned briefly in Chester F. Chapin, *Personification in Eighteenth-Century English Poetry* (1954; rpt. New York: Octagon, 1968), pp. 14–15. Chapin also lists a series of later critics, pro and con (pp. 137–138nn36,37). Though he considers only Addison and Johnson, Joseph H. Summers offers a fuller discussion in *The Muse's Method: An Introduction to "Paradise Lost"* (Cambridge, Mass.: Harvard University Press, 1962), pp. 33–39. In an indirect tribute to Addison's influence, editor John T. Shawcross mentions "the error of including the allegory of Sin and Death in the epic" as one of several "clichés inherited" by later critics from the early decades of the century (*Milton 1732–1801: The Critical Heritage*, Boston: Routledge and Kegan Paul, 1972, p. 1).

7. First in the *Spectator*, no. 273; then in nos. 309, 315, and 357 (II, 563–564; III, 119, 145–146, 336–337).

8. In this general form, Addison's objection reappears in John Hughes, "An Essay on Allegorical Poetry, &c." (1715), in *Critical Essays of the Eighteenth Century: 1700–1725*, ed. Willard Higley Durham (New Haven: Yale University Press, 1915), p. 95; John Lawson, *Lectures Concerning Oratory* (1758; rpt. in facsimile Menston, England: Scholar, 1969), p. 265; James Burnet (Lord Monboddo), *Of the Origin and Progress of Language*, III (1776, rpt. in facsimile Menston, England: Scholar, 1967), 150.

9. *Spectator*, nos. 273 (II, 563), 309 (III, 119, 120), 357 (III, 336).

10. *Spectator*, no. 419 (III, 570). For Addison's sense of "fiction" as it relates to allegorical personification, see Chapin, *Personification*, pp. 13–14, 19. Essentially, a "fiction" is a representation lacking any "pattern" in nature. In *Spectator*, no. 418, Addison distinguishes two poetic tasks: a poet can satisfy the imagination either "by mending and perfecting Nature where he describes a Reality," or "by adding greater Beauties than are put together in Nature, where he describes a Fiction" (III, 569). Addison is too much of an empiricist to imply that such fictions entirely break free of the natural; his remark that "the Poet quite loses sight of Nature" means only, according to Earl R. Wasserman, that "although he employs the materials of empirical reality, he employs them outside their normal, or 'natural,' context" ("The Inherent Values of Eighteenth-Century Personification," *PMLA*, 65, 1950, 443).

11. *Spectator*, no. 419 (III, 573).

12. *Spectator,* no. 419 (III, 570, 572–573). Addison refers to Ovid's Envy (*Metamorphoses,* II.768ff) and Hunger (VIII.799ff); and to Virgil's Fame (*Aeneid,* IV.175ff). Without attempting a count, I would guess that Virgil's figure is more frequently cited by eighteenth-century critics than any other instance of personification; we will encounter it repeatedly in this book.

13. *Spectator,* no. 297 (III, 60). Addison's attempt to identify the classical regularities, as opposed to the "romantic" excrescences, of *Paradise Lost* continues a long tradition of debate over the application of Aristotelian criteria to the Renaissance epic. The debate had its origins in the efforts of sixteenth-century Italian criticism to assimilate the "epics" of Dante and Ariosto; see for example the selections from Cinthio, Minturno, and Mazzoni in *Literary Criticism: Plato to Dryden,* ed. Allen H. Gilbert (1940; rpt. Detroit: Wayne State University Press, 1962), pp. 262–273, 275–289, 359.

14. Hughes, "Essay on Allegorical Poetry," pp. 88, 91–92, 95.

15. Richard Hurd, *Letters on Chivalry and Romance,* ed. Hoyt Trowbridge (1762; rpt. in facsimile Los Angeles: William Andrews Clark Memorial Library, 1963), p. 57.

16. Ibid., pp. 117–118.

17. *Spectator,* no. 297 (III, 60).

18. *Spectator,* no. 315 (III, 144–146).

19. M. H. Abrams, *The Mirror and the Lamp: Romantic Theory and the Critical Tradition* (New York: Oxford University Press, 1953), p. 267. For Aristotle's emphasis on probability even when at the expense of possibility, see *Poetics,* chap. 24, in *The Basic Works of Aristotle,* ed. Richard McKeon (New York: Random House, 1941), p. 1482.

20. *Spectator,* no. 273 (II, 563).

21. The term "internalization" as applied to poetry written after Milton inevitably alludes to the numerous writings of Harold Bloom.

22. François Marie Arouet de Voltaire, "Milton," in *An Essay Upon the Civil Wars of France . . . And also Upon the Epick Poetry of the European Nations, from Homer down to Milton,* 4th ed. (London, 1731), p. 78; Samuel Johnson, *Lives of the English Poets,* ed. George Birkbeck Hill (1905; rpt. New York: Octagon, 1967), I, 181.

23. *Spectator,* no. 273 (II, 563).

24. *Spectator,* no. 357 (III, 330, 336–337).

25. *The Iliad of Homer,* trans. Richard Lattimore (Chicago: University of Chicago Press, 1951), p. 236.

26. *Spectator,* no. 321 (III, 173).

27. *The Iliad,* p. 125. Once again, Eris seems equivalent to a goddess; her activities in this episode are shared by Ares and Athene. Indeed, she is Ares' sister. Here is Pope's version of the whole passage:

Each Host now joins, and each a God inspires,
These *Mars* incites, and those *Minerva* fires.
Pale *Flight* around, and dreadful *Terror* reign,

And *Discord* raging bathes the purple Plain:
Discord! dire Sister of the slaught'ring Pow'r,
Small at her Birth, but rising ev'ry Hour,
While scarce the Skies her horrid Head can bound,
She stalks on Earth, and shakes the World around;
The Nations bleed, where-e'er her Steps she turns,
The Groan still deepens, and the Combate burns.

Pope's lines are quoted from *The Twickenham Edition of the Poems of Alexander Pope*, VII, ed. Maynard Mack (New Haven: Yale University Press, 1967), 244–245. Despite his full "realization" of Discord here—and his willingness to designate the god of war almost allegorically as "the slaught'ring Pow'r"— Pope nevertheless distinguishes, like Addison, between gods and allegorical agents. His "Poetical Index to *Homer's Iliad*" includes a list of "Allegorical or Fictitious Persons in Homer." Rather than among the "Characters of the Gods," Discord (Eris) is listed here, along with Fame, the Furies, Discord (Ate), Bellona, the Hours, Death, Sleep, and others (*Twickenham Edition*, VIII, ed. Maynard Mack, 1967, 592).

28. The reversibility of allegorical agency is one topic of Angus Fletcher's fine chapter "The Daemonic Agent," in his *Allegory: The Theory of a Symbolic Mode* (Ithaca: Cornell University Press, 1964), pp. 25–69. Commenting on the personified abstraction, Fletcher writes: "This personifying process has a reverse type, in which the poet treats real people in a formulaic way so that they become walking Ideas" (pp. 27–28). A clear instance is the transformation of Malbecco in the *Faerie Queene* (III.ix–x) from an "eminently real and natural and comic" jealous husband into the grotesquely isolated personification of "Gealosie" (pp. 49–50).

29. I use "metaphor" here in a very general sense; the precise rhetorical origins of personification are various, even in a single case. The still indispensable terms "tenor" and "vehicle" were introduced by I. A. Richards in *The Philosophy of Rhetoric* (1936; rpt. New York: Oxford University Press, 1965), p. 96.

30. Henry Home (Lord Kames), *Elements of Criticism*, 6th ed. (1785; rpt. in facsimile New York: Garland, 1972), II, 293. Joshua Reynolds, reluctantly conceding Rubens' practice of mixing "allegorical figures with representations of real personages . . . to be a fault," nevertheless reverses Kames in asserting the superiority of allegorical painting. While allegorical poetry has often been called "tedious, and uninteresting," the multiplicity of figures in allegorical painting "produces a greater variety of ideal beauty, a richer, more various and delightful composition, and gives to the artist a greater opportunity of exhibiting his skill" (*Discourses on Art*, London: Collier, 1959, Discourse 7, pp. 114–115; Kames's *Elements* first appeared in 1762; Reynolds' seventh discourse was delivered in 1776.) Reynolds' ambivalence toward Rubens' mixed allegory clearly parallels Addison's ambivalence toward Milton's Sin and Death.

Kames's preference for literary personifications was shared by Edmund Burke, though for a different reason. The obscurity of such figures as Virgil's Fame and Homer's Discord is what, according to Burke, produces their magnificence: "These figures in painting would be clear enough, but I fear they might become ridiculous" (*PE*, p. 64).

31. Kames, *Elements*, II, 386–387.

32. Ibid., II, 228–235.

33. Ibid., II, 393–395. *Pace* Chapin, who lists Kames among the critics sharing Addison's rejection of Sin and Death (*Personification*, p. 138n37).

34. *Spectator*, no. 273 (II, 564). In contrast to both Addison and Kames, John Dennis calls attention to the extravagant length, as opposed to the seemly brevity, of Virgil's description of Fame, "who is drawn in fifteen Lines at length; three of which Number describe her Person." In further contrast to Kames, who considers Fame acceptable because she is only "a description," Dennis allows the description only because Fame is such an important agent: "we are to consider the importance of that Machine; which causes the Departure of *Aeneas*, and the Death of *Dido*; which are two of the most considerable Events of the Poem" ("Remarks on a Book Entitled, Prince Arthur," 1696, in *Critical Works of John Dennis*, ed. Edward Niles Hooker, I, Baltimore: Johns Hopkins University Press, 1939, 106). But Dennis is clearly thinking of Fame as a literal supernatural agent—not as a personification.

35. *Spectator*, no. 357 (III, 337, 338).

36. Patricia Meyer Spacks discusses Johnson and Kames together as notable opponents of unrestricted personification; see *The Insistence of Horror: Aspects of the Supernatural in Eighteenth-Century Poetry* (Cambridge, Mass.: Harvard University Press, 1962), pp. 169–171.

37. Johnson, *Lives*, I, 185–186. Johnson's opinion of Sin and Death is of course consonant with his general rejection of poetic machinery. His contempt most frequently falls on modern poets who show their insincerity by dabbling in classical mythology; see *Lives*, I, 213, 295, 338, 462; II, 16, 68, 283, 294, 311; III, 228, 291, 439. Taken together with Johnson's famous assault on *Lycidas* (I, 163–165), such remarks amount almost to a Romantic promotion of sincerity; cf. Walter Jackson Bate, *Samuel Johnson* (New York: Harcourt Brace Jovanovich, 1977), p. 538. Granting full weight to contrary tendencies in Johnson's criticism, William Edinger has recently argued a case for viewing Johnson as a precursor of Wordsworth on poetic diction in his *Samuel Johnson and Poetic Style* (Chicago: University of Chicago Press, 1977), esp. pp. 172–176. In his emphasis on Johnson's empiricism, Edinger follows Jean H. Hagstrum, *Samuel Johnson's Literary Criticism* (Chicago: University of Chicago Press, 1952).

38. *Spectator*, no. 357 (III, 338).

39. *Life of Pope*, in Johnson, *Lives*, III, 233.

40. I take the term "static agency" from Fletcher, *Allegory*, p. 66.

41. Johnson, *Lives*, I, 183, 181.

3. Sublime Personification

1. Bertrand H. Bronson, "Personification Reconsidered," *ELH*, 14 (1947), 163–177; Earl R. Wasserman, "The Inherent Values of Eighteenth-Century Personification," *PMLA*, 65 (1950), 435–463; Chester F. Chapin, *Personification in Eighteenth-Century English Poetry* (1954; rpt. New York: Octagon, 1974).

2. This is not to deny the usefulness of many additional studies, including Norman Maclean, "From Action to Image: Theories of the Lyric in the Eighteenth Century," in *Critics and Criticism: Ancient and Modern*, ed. R. S. Crane (Chicago: University of Chicago Press, 1952), pp. 439–445; Donald Davie, *Purity of Diction in English Verse* (New York: Oxford University Press, 1953), pp. 35–47; Rachel Trickett, "The Augustan Pantheon: Mythology and Personification in Eighteenth Century Poetry," *Essays and Studies*, n.s. 6 (1953), 71–86; Jean Hagstrum, *The Sister Arts: The Tradition of Literary Pictorialism and English Poetry from Dryden to Gray* (Chicago: University of Chicago Press, 1958); Patricia Meyer Spacks, *The Insistence of Horror: Aspects of the Supernatural in Eighteenth-Century Poetry* (Cambridge, Mass.: Harvard University Press, 1962), chaps. 5 and 6; Kurt Schlüter, *Die Englische Ode: Studien zu Ihrer Entwicklung unter dem Einfluss der Antiken Hymne* (Bonn: H. Bouvier, 1964), esp. chap. 6; John E. Sitter, "Mother, Memory, Muse and Poetry after Pope," *ELH*, 44 (1977), 312–336. Sitter's treatment of the theme of poetic ambition and Spacks's survey of "horror-personification" are important resources for studying the relation between personification and the sublime. Angus Fletcher specifically addresses the topic of personification in his *Allegory: The Theory of a Symbolic Mode* (Ithaca: Cornell University Press, 1964), pp. 26–35, and his entire chapter "The Daemonic Agent" (pp. 25–69) is relevant. Valuable remarks on personification occur frequently in the essays of Geoffrey H. Hartman; see his collections *Beyond Formalism: Literary Essays, 1958–1970* (New Haven: Yale University Press, 1970) and *The Fate of Reading and Other Essays* (Chicago: University of Chicago Press, 1975).

3. Cf. the discussion of Longinus in William K. Wimsatt, Jr. and Cleanth Brooks, *Literary Criticism: A Short History* (New York: Random House, 1957), p. 104. Wimsatt complains of the difficulty of knowing whether Longinus refers to "something observable in the poem itself—or something outside the poem which causes the poem—or again something which the poem causes in its audience." Neil Hertz takes this problem as the starting point for his penetrating essay "A Reading of Longinus," *Critical Inquiry*, 9 (1983), 579–596.

4. Wasserman, "Inherent Values," pp. 441–442, quoting *The Poetical Works of William Collins*, ed. Mrs. A. L. Barbauld (London, 1797), p. vii.

5. For discussions of Burke's treatment of Milton's Death, see the beginnings of Chapters 1 and 2.

6. *Dionysius Longinus on the Sublime*, trans. William Smith, 3rd ed. (London, 1752), pp. 3–4. I quote from an influential eighteenth-century transla-

tion. Boileau's earlier and even more important translation makes the emphasis on the speaker himself more distinct: "Mais quand le Sublime vient à paroistre où il faut; il renverse tout comme un foudre, & presente d'abord toutes les forces de l'Orateur ramassées ensemble" ("Traité du sublime," in Nicholas Boileau-Despréaux, *Oeuvres diverses,* Paris, 1674, p. 5).

7. *Dionysius Longinus on the Sublime,* p. 21. This principle of identification allows Longinus not only to connect the orator with the audience (or the poet with the reader), but also to translate the rhetorical power of a fiction into the inventive power of its author. Hertz, in "A Reading of Longinus," focuses on the complex role played by such shifting identifications in Longinus' argument. He also reminds us of the eighteenth-century habit of repeating such identifications in commentary on Longinus himself: "To say, with Boileau and Pope, that Longinus 'is himself the great Sublime he draws,' or to profess to doubt, as Gibbon did, 'which is the most sublime, Homer's Battle of the Gods or Longinus' apostrophe . . . upon it,' is knowingly to override certain conventional lines of demarcation . . . very much in the manner of Longinus overriding the distinction between Homer and his heroes, between sublime language and its author . . . or between sublime poet and his audience" (p. 579).

8. Such occasions do in fact abound in Longinus, nearly all of whose main examples are violent, but Longinus never makes violence an explicit criterion of sublimity.

9. Boulton's Introduction to *PE* gives a balanced account of the ways in which Burke's emphasis on terror partly derived from and partly reoriented contemporary attitudes toward the sublime.

10. *Gibbon's Journal: To January 28th, 1763,* ed. D. M. Low (London: Chatto and Windus, 1929), p. 180 (entry for October 4, 1762).

11. Thomas Green, *Extracts from the Diary of a Lover of Literature* (Ipswich, 1810), p. 48 (entry for October 18, 1797).

12. Another reference appears in the Preface to Burke's first edition. But Longinus is a submerged presence elsewhere in *PE;* see for example pp. 64 and 143, where Burke adopts literary examples already singled out by Longinus.

13. Samuel H. Monk, *The Sublime: A Study of Critical Theories in XVIII-Century England* (New York: Modern Language Association, 1935), pp. 4–9.

14. *CAJ,* pp. 98, 106; *IKW,* V, 322, 329.

15. *CAJ,* pp. 110–111; *IKW,* V, 332–334. Meredith's phrase *"picturing to ourselves"* is, unfortunately, more colorful than the original; Kant merely says that we *think (denken)* of what it would be like to resist the power of the fearful object.

16. *CAJ,* pp. 111–112; *IKW,* V, 334.

17. Thomas Weiskel, *The Romantic Sublime: Studies in the Structure and Psychology of Transcendence* (Baltimore: Johns Hopkins University Press, 1976), pp. 40–41.

18. Weiskel notes the role of personification in his own argument (*The Romantic Sublime,* pp. 66, 85).

19. Ibid., pp. 41, 92–97.

20. Neil Hertz, "The Notion of Blockage in the Literature of the Sublime," in *Psychoanalysis and the Question of the Text, Selected Papers from the English Institute, 1976–77,* ed. Geoffrey H. Hartman (Baltimore: Johns Hopkins University Press, 1978), pp. 71–76; Hertz also follows up on Weiskel's hints about the artificiality of the oedipal model (pp. 103–106).

21. Hertz, "Blockage," p. 76.

22. Ibid., p. 76.

23. *CAJ,* p. 112; *IKW,* V, 334.

24. *CAJ,* pp. 113–114; *IKW,* V, 335–336.

25. *CAJ,* pp. 115–116; *IKW,* V, 337.

26. In its most radical moments, the Kantian dualism of agency denies all possibility of contact between empirical and genuine moral agency: "In actual fact it is absolutely impossible for experience to establish with complete certainty a single case in which the maxim of an action . . . has rested solely on moral grounds and on the thought of one's duty." Kant is thus willing to doubt "whether any genuine virtue is actually to be encountered in this world" (*Groundwork of the Metaphysic of Morals,* trans. H. J. Paton, 3rd ed., 1956; rpt. New York: Harper and Row, 1964, pp. 74–75; cf. *Critique of Pure Reason,* trans. Norman Kemp Smith, 1929; rpt. New York: St. Martin's, 1965, p. 275).

27. *CAJ,* p. 128; *IKW,* V, 347. Elsewhere, in a discussion of religious illusion, Kant offers the following distinction between fanaticism and superstition: "It is a superstitious illusion *(abergläubischer Wahn)* to wish to become well-pleasing to God through actions which anyone can perform without even needing to be a good man . . . But an illusion is called fanatical *(schwärmerisch)* when the very means it contemplates, as supersensible, are not within man's power, leaving out of account the inaccessibility of the supersensible end aimed at by these means; for this feeling of the immediate presence of the Supreme Being . . . would constitute a receptivity for an intuition *(Anschauung)* for which there is no sensory provision in man's nature." And this substitution of an empirical intuition for "basic principles" amounts to "the moral death of reason" (*Religion within the Limits of Reason Alone,* trans. Theodore M. Greene and Hoyt H. Hudson, 1934; rpt. New York: Harper and Row, 1960, pp. 162–163; *IKW,* VI, 324–325). For Kant, the speculative aggrandizement of cognition always tends toward *Schwärmerei;* his favorite example in philosophy is Spinoza. See Thomas McFarland, *Coleridge and the Pantheist Tradition* (Oxford: Clarendon, 1969), pp. 90–91.

28. Weiskel, *The Romantic Sublime,* pp. 40–41.

29. *CAJ,* pp. 127–128; *IKW,* V, 347. The end of this quotation directly precedes the passage on fanaticism cited by Weiskel (*The Romantic Sublime,* p. 41) as evidence of the imagination's passivity.

30. *CAJ,* p. 128; *IKW,* V, 347–348. Kant earlier glosses his distinction between "affection" *(Affekt)* and "passion" *(Leidenschaft)* as follows: "Affec-

tions are related merely to feeling; passions belong to the faculty of desire . . . Affections are impetuous and irresponsible: passions are abiding and deliberate. Thus resentment, in the form of anger, is an affection: but in the form of hatred (vindictiveness) it is a passion. Under no circumstances can the latter be called sublime; for, while the freedom of the mind is, no doubt, *impeded* in the case of affection, in passion it is abrogated" (*CAJ*, p. 124n; *IKW*, V, 344n). Cf. the similar distinction made by Coleridge in his discussion of poetic violence in his "Apologetic Preface" (see Chapter 1).

31. Such ambivalence is the moral equivalent of a cognitive oscillation in the mathematical sublime: "The mind feels itself *set in motion* in the representation of the sublime . . . This movement . . . may be compared with a vibration *(Erschütterung)*, i.e. with a rapidly alternating repulsion and attraction to one and the same Object. The point of excess for the imagination (towards which it is driven in the apprehension of the intuition) is like an abyss in which it fears to lose itself" (*CAJ*, p. 107; *IKW*, V, 329–330).

32. *Prolegomena to Any Future Metaphysics*, ed., from earlier translations, by Lewis White Beck (New York: Bobbs-Merrill, 1950), p. 8. Kant's empiricism is a frequent target of criticism by idealists; a modern Hegelian, J. N. Findlay, credits Hegel with having "laid bare the crypto-empiricism which haunts the thought of Kant" (Foreword to *Hegel's Logic*, trans. William Wallace, 3rd ed., Oxford: Clarendon, 1975, p. xii).

33. *MC*, p. 39. The emphasis on "borrowed" is added; that on "appear" is Coleridge's. For an answer to Coleridge's criticism from the perspective of Renaissance poetics, see Paul Alpers, *The Poetry of "The Faerie Queene"* (Princeton: Princeton University Press, 1967), p. 11.

34. Cf. C. S. Lewis on Lucifera's counsellors (*Faerie Queene*, I.iv.18–35): "Each . . . has a mortal disease" (*The Allegory of Love: A Study in Medieval Tradition*, London: Oxford University Press, 1936, p. 315).

35. Spacks, *The Insistence of Horror*, pp. 156–157.

36. Spacks, *The Insistence of Horror*, p. 157, quoting *James Thomson, 1700–1748: Letters and Documents*, ed. Alan Dugald McKillop (Lawrence: University of Kansas Press, 1958), p. 44.

37. Spacks, *The Insistence of Horror*, pp. 157–158.

38. Two relevant instances—Salvator Rosa's *Democritus in Meditation* (1662) and an anonymous portrait of Pope after the poet's own design (1730's)— are reproduced in John Dixon Hunt, *The Figure in the Landscape: Poetry, Painting, and Gardening during the Eighteenth Century* (Baltimore: Johns Hopkins University Press, 1976), Plates 25 and 33 (pp. 46, 61). Rosa's Democritus leans against a broken wall, brooding over a pile of human and animal remains; on the left are an urn and two ruined obelisks; an owl is perched on a forked branch in the upper left corner. In the other portrait Pope sits before the legs of a shattered statue, the head and shoulders of which lie at his feet; a skull is poised on a broken wall, above the poet's own head; the background is dominated by a truncated column and a ruined coliseum. The *locus classicus* for such figures is of course Dürer's *Melencolia I*.

39. Harold Bloom, *The Anxiety of Influence: A Theory of Poetry* (New

York: Oxford University Press, 1973), pp. 110–111; Weiskel, *The Romantic Sublime*, chap. 5; Paul S. Sherwin, *Precious Bane: Collins and the Miltonic Legacy* (Austin: University of Texas Press, 1977); Paul H. Fry, *The Poet's Calling in the English Ode* (New Haven: Yale University Press, 1980), chap. 5. Prior to this psychoanalytic tradition, the view of Collins as a lone exemplar of Romantic imagination was most forcefully argued in A. S. P. Woodhouse's two classic essays "Collins and the Creative Imagination: A Study in the Critical Background of His Odes (1746)," in *Studies in English by Members of University College, Toronto*, ed. M. W. Wallace (Toronto: University of Toronto Press, 1931), pp. 59–130, and "The Poetry of Collins Reconsidered," in *From Sensibility to Romanticism: Essays Presented to Frederick A. Pottle*, ed. Frederick W. Hilles and Harold Bloom (New York: Oxford University Press, 1965), pp. 93–137.

40. For recent expressions of dissent from the psychoanalytic view, see Marshall Brown, "The Urbane Sublime," *ELH*, 45 (1978), 246–247; Richard Wendorf, *William Collins and Eighteenth-Century English Poetry* (Minneapolis: University of Minnesota Press, 1981); and, from a de Manian rhetorical perspective, Janice Haney-Peritz, " 'In Quest of Mistaken Beauties': Allegorical Indeterminacy in Collins' Poetry," *ELH*, 48 (1981), 732–756.

41. *The Works of William Collins*, ed. Richard Wendorf and Charles Ryskamp (Oxford: Clarendon, 1979), p. 27. While quoting from this edition, I will also be citing Roger Lonsdale's excellent commentary in his *Poems of Thomas Gray, William Collins, and Oliver Goldsmith* (London: Longman, 1969).

42. Earlier readers have noticed Fear's reflexiveness; two earlier accounts, differing from each other and from the one presented here, are provided by Sherwin (*Precious Bane*, pp. 64–66) and Wendorf (*William Collins*, pp. 102–103).

43. On Collins' relation to the tradition of "odes for music," see Wendorf, *William Collins*, chap. 6.

44. Lonsdale, *Poems of Gray, Collins, and Goldsmith*, p. 480n.

45. *The Poems of Sir Philip Sidney*, ed. William A. Ringler, Jr. (Oxford: Clarendon, 1962), p. 145.

46. *The Works of Edmund Spenser: A Variorum Edition*, ed. Edwin Greenlaw et al., 9 vols. (Baltimore: Johns Hopkins University Press, 1932–1949), I, 21.

47. For the entire incident, see Ovid, *Metamorphoses*, XI.1–60. The objects are at first enchanted by Orpheus' music and will not allow themselves to be used against him until the Bacchantes drown out the music with their own howling. Milton mentions the "Woods and Rocks" that "had Ears / To rapture, till the savage clamor drown'd / Both Harp and Voice," but his highly condensed allusion omits their role in Orpheus' destruction.

48. Cf. Brown, "The Urbane Sublime," p. 247: "*The Passions* passes the tragic emotions in view only in order to let each refute itself: thus, Fear recoils in fear, Anger is too impatient to remain, Despair 'beguiles' itself, and so forth."

49. The "Ode to Peace," written between June and December 1746, might be a third response to the rebellion, but Lonsdale plausibly argues that its appeal for an honorable peace "would not have been appropriate to the Young Pretender's invasion, so the poem probably refers to the war with France" (*Poems of Gray, Collins, and Goldsmith*, p. 467 headnote).

50. *The Twickenham Edition of the Poems of Alexander Pope*, V, ed. James Sutherland, 3rd ed. (New Haven: Yale University Press, 1963), 331–332; 1743 version, III.235–252. Further prophecies include a vision of Cibber himself mounting the wind on "grinning dragons." Pope's annotation alludes to the common practice of justifying extravagant fictions by pleading an allegorical intention: "In his Letter to Mr. P. Mr. C. solemnly declares this not to be *literally true*. We hope therefore the reader will understand it *allegorically* only" (p. 333n). Cibberian dulness might thus be said to anticipate both sides of the sublime ambivalence, as an unsympathetic observer would perceive it: deluded amazement at one's own inventions, and a (pathetic) appeal to the distinction between literal and fictional belief. Cibber is forced into a role not far from the one Coleridge adopts in his "Apologetic Preface."

51. See Lonsdale's headnote to "Ode to Pity" (*Poems of Gray, Collins, and Goldsmith*, pp. 414–415) and the fuller account of the unfinished translation in Wendorf and Ryskamp, *Works of William Collins*, pp. 212–214. For an account of the relation between the sublime and eighteenth-century and Romantic theories of tragedy, see W. P. Albrecht, *The Sublime Pleasures of Tragedy: A Study of Critical Theory from Dennis to Keats* (Lawrence: University of Kansas Press, 1975).

52. Lonsdale, *Poems of Gray, Collins, and Goldsmith*, p. 421n.

53. On "imagined stage scenes" in Collins, see John R. Crider, "Structure and Effect in Collins' Progress Poems," *Studies in Philology*, 60 (1963), 61–62. The theatrical, even "histrionic" character of much mid-century literature provides the starting point for Martin Price's chapter "The Theatre of Mind," in his *To the Palace of Wisdom: Studies in Order and Energy from Dryden to Blake* (Carbondale and Edwardsville: Southern Illinois University Press, 1964), chap. 12.

54. But it occurs thirty times, counting plurals, in Collins' small poetic corpus; see Bradford A. Booth and Claude E. Jones, *A Concordance of the Poetical Works of William Collins* (Berkeley: University of California Press, 1939), p. 88.

55. The reticence of Collins' line can be seen by comparing a line from Pope, suggested by Lonsdale (*Poems of Gray, Collins, and Goldsmith*, p. 419n): "There purple *Vengeance* bath'd in Gore retires" (*Windsor-Forest*, l. 417). Lonsdale goes on to list examples of red arms in Horace, Milton, Dryden, Pope, and Broome, but the references are to God or Jove, not to a female monster. See Weiskel, *The Romantic Sublime*, p. 113, for an intriguing psychoanalytic reading of this switch in genders.

56. On the importance and typicality of "movement into a sacred precinct" in the poetry of Collins and his contemporaries, see Martin Price, "The

Sublime Poem: Pictures and Powers," *Yale Review,* n.s. 58 (1968–1969), 199–201.

57. *Oedipus at Colonus,* trans. Robert Fitzgerald, in *Sophocles I,* ed. David Greene and Richard Lattimore (Chicago: University of Chicago Press, 1954), ll. 1622–1628, p. 149.

58. Weiskel, viewing Collins' "mistake" from a psychoanalytic perspective, understandably concludes, "Had Freud never lived, we would be driven to the hypothesis of the oedipal complex to make sense of these lines" (*The Romantic Sublime,* p. 116). A memory distortion of this magnitude and with this particular content—replacing a father-god with an incestuous mother, turning death (not to mention blinding, that is, castration) into incestuous consummation—*should* strike a psychoanalyst as unusually revelatory. At the same time, however, it ought to strike him as too good to be true—at least it should raise the queston of how so blatant an expression of a forbidden wish fits into a text as polite, artificial, and public as Collins' poem.

59. In his important essay "False Themes and Gentle Minds," Geoffrey H. Hartman remarks that Collins and other writers in the Age of Sensibility could "risk" invoking sublime personifications "because they knew the Enlightenment had gone too far for the old superstitions really to come back" (*Beyond Formalism,* p. 291). My somewhat different claim is that Collins' flirtation with archaic beliefs is intended to dramatize, or rather to produce, an impossible freedom from literal belief as such.

4. Wordsworth and the Limits of Allegory

1. Long after being struck by the self-absorption of personified abstractions, I encountered Michael Fried's fascinating study *Absorption and Theatricality: Painting and Beholder in the Age of Diderot* (Berkeley: University of California Press, 1980). While the points of contact between Fried's argument and this one are too complex and numerous to record here, his book confirms my sense of the importance of self-enclosed agency in eighteenth-century art in various media.

2. On the relation of sublime personification to Pope's *Dunciad,* see John E. Sitter, "Mother, Memory, Muse and Poetry after Pope," *ELH,* 44 (1977), 312–336. The proximity of the sublime to satire is intriguingly discussed by Thomas Weiskel in *The Romantic Sublime: Studies in the Structure and Psychology of Transcendence* (Baltimore: Johns Hopkins University Press, 1976), pp. 19–20. For an attempt to reconcile Augustan satire and post-Augustan sublime poetry under a broader notion of urbane discourse, see Marshall Brown, "The Urbane Sublime," *ELH,* 45 (1978), 236–254.

3. Jonathan Wordsworth gathers these figures together under the inevitable generic title of "borderers." See his lecture "William Wordsworth, 1770–1969," *Proceedings of the British Academy,* 55 (1969), 211–228; see also his *William Wordsworth: The Borders of Vision* (Oxford: Clarendon, 1982).

4. *The Prelude: 1799, 1805, 1850,* ed. Jonathan Wordsworth, M. H. Abrams, and Stephen Gill (New York: Norton, 1979), p. 260; 1805 version, VII.610–623. All quotations of *The Prelude* are from this edition and are given hereafter in the text by year, book, and line. For a full reading of the Blind Beggar passage and its context in the London episode, see Neil Hertz, "The Notion of Blockage in the Literature of the Sublime," in *Psychoanalysis and the Question of the Text, Selected Papers from the English Institute, 1976–77,* ed. Geoffrey H. Hartman (Baltimore: Johns Hopkins University Press, 1978), pp. 79–84.

5. *BL,* II, 138. I quote Wordsworth's passage as it appears in Coleridge's text; subsequent references to these lines are based on the standard text in *PWW,* IV, 282.

My treatment of Coleridge's critique of this passage ignores the complexities of Coleridge's personal ambivalences both toward Wordsworth and toward philosophical children. But see Thomas McFarland, "Wordsworth's Best Philosopher," *Wordsworth Circle,* 13 (1982), 64–68, for the intriguing thesis that Wordsworth modeled his apostrophe to the Child on Coleridge's manner of praising the intellect of his own infant son Hartley.

6. In a different context, Frances Ferguson writes evocatively on the effect of personifying what are already persons; see *Wordsworth: Language as Counter-Spirit* (New Haven: Yale University Press, 1977), pp. 26–28.

7. *The Works of William Collins,* ed. Richard Wendorf and Charles Ryskamp (Oxford: Clarendon, 1979), pp. 25, 29, 35, 46, 27.

8. From this perspective, Ferguson's plausible claim (*Wordsworth,* p. 27) that Wordsworth equated "most personifications" with idolatry needs qualifying.

9. Cf. Wordsworth's call, in the first "Essay upon Epitaphs" (1810), for a "spiritualizing" abstractness in representations of the deceased (*PrW,* I, 56–59).

10. On the resemblance of this episode to the Kantian sublime, see Weiskel, *The Romantic Sublime,* pp. 42–44; but see also his more complex treatment, pp. 195–204.

11. The episode has, naturally, elicited psychoanalytic commentary; see Leslie Brisman's intriguing account in *Romantic Origins* (Ithaca: Cornell University Press, 1978), pp. 314–318.

12. Peter is not the only one gazing into the water; the dead man's faithful Ass stands "close by Peter's side" (562) and looks on eagerly as Peter probes the corpse before entwining his sapling in its hair (556–570). There are two figures, then, one of which watches as the other stirs—just as the poet in "Resolution and Independence" stands beside the stirring Leech-Gatherer. The Ass, furthermore, is in various ways similar to the Leech-Gatherer: he is oddly stationary, mysterious, and solitary when Peter first notices him hanging "his head / Over the silent stream" (385–395). In short, as John E. Jordan remarks, the Ass is another of Wordsworth's "borderers,"

another of the beings "inhabiting realms between the expected" ("Words-worth's Most Wonderful as Well as Most Admirable Poem," *Wordsworth Circle,* 10, 1979, 51).

13. *Journals of Dorothy Wordsworth,* ed. Ernest de Selincourt (London: Macmillan, 1941), I, 63 (entry for October 3, 1800).

14. Lewis Carroll (Charles Lutwidge Dodgson), *Through the Looking Glass,* in *The Complete Works of Lewis Carroll* (New York: Modern Library–Random House, 1936), pp. 246–247.

15. Geoffrey H. Hartman, *Wordsworth's Poetry, 1789–1814* (New Haven: Yale University Press, 1964), p. 269.

16. George Wilbur Meyer long ago suggested that Wordsworth's anxious poet was actually modeled on Coleridge and not on Wordsworth himself (*"Resolution and Independence:* Wordsworth's Answer to Coleridge's *Dejection: An Ode," Tulane Studies in English,* 2, 1950, 68–69).

17. My argument goes against the tendency to assign the Leech-Gatherer a genuinely therapeutic role in relation to the speaker or to Wordsworth himself. According to Frank Kermode, for example, "What saves the poet . . . is the symbol-making power; it is not what the Leech Gatherer says, but the fact that Wordsworth could invent him, that saves his joy and his sanity, gives him victory" (*Romantic Image,* London: Routledge and Kegan Paul, 1957, p. 11). More recently, Peter J. Manning has written that "Wordsworth purges himself of his 'untoward thoughts' (l. 53) by splitting them off and embodying them in the Leech-gatherer" (" 'My former thoughts returned': Wordsworth's *Resolution and Independence," Wordsworth Circle,* 9, 1978, 401). An opposite but equally therapeutic reading locates the value of the Leech-Gatherer not in his status as a projection of the poet's own psyche but in his capacity to resist the poet's projections; thus Michael G. Cooke argues that the Old Man compels the poet to "a lucid recognition of the intrinsic state and force of what meets him" (*The Romantic Will,* New Haven: Yale University Press, 1976, p. 211); cf. Weiskel, *The Romantic Sublime,* p. 139. But also see Weiskel, p. 33, for the suggestion that the poem's power may, in fact, have more to do with the "unrelenting agency" of its "Spenserian cadences" than with the psychological "career" of its protagonist.

18. For this reason I am skeptical of Samuel E. Schulman's intriguing attempt to read the poem in terms of a complex evocation of moral themes from Spenser ("The Spenserian Enchantments of Wordsworth's 'Resolution and Independence,' " *Modern Philology,* 79, 1981, 24–44). Schulman finds, as I do, that the "Spenserian voice, lodged so queerly with the leech-gatherer, is above all a detached voice," but I cannot accept his thematic claim that it is "a voice that can be deployed at will to triumph over mere appearances, to lie, and to clothe the naked simplicity of the old man's narrative" (p. 40). But I am indebted to Schulman for pointing out the Leech-Gatherer's close resemblance to Spenser's Ignaro (pp. 36–38).

19. *PWW,* I, 270–283. A sample from the poem, ll. 387–396 (p. 279):

Ha! that is hell-born Murder nigh
With haggard, half-reverted eye,
And now aghast he seems to stare
On some strange Vision in the air,
And Suicide with savage glance
Started from his brooding trance,
Then sunk again, anon he eyed
With sullen smiles the torpid tide;
And moody Madness aye was there
With wide-rent robe, and shaggy hair.

In originally autobiographical lines transferred to the portrait of the Wanderer in *The Excursion* (I.180–184; *PWW*, V, 14), Wordsworth mentions his early attraction to the Gothic figures in an ancient volume

Profuse in garniture of wooden cuts
Strange and uncouth; dire faces, figures dire,
Sharp-kneed, sharp-elbowed, and lean-ankled too,
With long and ghostly shanks—forms which once seen
Could never be forgotten!

20. And here was Labour, his own Bond-slave; Hope
That never set the pains against the prize;
Idleness, halting with his weary clog;
And poor misguided Shame, and witless Fear,
And simple Pleasure, foraging for Death . . .

—and so on, for nine additional lines.

21. My remarks on this poem are indebted to two important commentaries: Michael Riffaterre, "Interpretation and Descriptive Poetry: A Reading of Wordsworth's 'Yew-Trees,' " *New Literary History*, 4 (1972–1973), 229–256; and Geoffrey H. Hartman, "The Use and Abuse of Structural Analysis: Riffaterre's Interpretation of Wordsworth's 'Yew-Trees,' " *New Literary History*, 7 (1975–1976), 165–189. As its title indicates, Hartman's article is in part a response to Riffaterre's impressively detailed treatment of the poem's formal structure; Hartman criticizes Riffaterre for suppressing the role of the poem's implied speaking subject, and, consequently, missing the force of its historical specificity. For another critique of Riffaterre, pressing the same issue on technical linguistic grounds, see Frederick Bowers, "Reference and Deixis in Wordsworth's 'Yew-Trees,' " *English Studies in Canada*, 5 (1979), 292–300.

22. Cf. Hartman, "Use and Abuse," p. 167.

23. Cf. Riffaterre, "Interpretation and Descriptive Poetry," p. 240: "This circularity (acting-acted upon) makes the solitariness of the tree look like a microcosm, or at the very least a space marked out by sacred confines."

24. On the poem's gradual approach to full personification, see Cleanth Brooks and Robert Penn Warren, *Understanding Poetry,* 3rd ed. (New York: Holt, Rinehart, and Winston, 1960), pp. 277–278.

25. Riffaterre, "Interpretation and Descriptive Poetry," p. 254. The quoted remark is, however, only part of what Riffaterre has to say about the personifications; he also provides a complex account of their grammatical status and thematic associations.

26. Hartman, "Use and Abuse," pp. 167, 169.

27. Ibid., pp. 169, 171.

28. *The Aeneid of Virgil,* trans. Allen Mandelbaum (New York: Bantam, 1972), p. 142.

29. *The Works of Edmund Spenser: A Variorum Edition,* ed. Edwin Greenlaw et al., 9 vols. (Baltimore: Johns Hopkins University Press, 1932–1949), II, 83–84. In Dante's *Inferno,* various guardian monsters—part mythological, part allegorical—are stationed at separate posts along the route to the center of Hell. Thus Minos, serpent-tailed like Milton's Sin, stands at the entrance to the second circle (Canto V); Cerberus torments the shades in the third circle (VI); Pluto waits at the turning point between circles three and four (VI and VII); the Furies threaten the pilgrims from the high watchtower of Dis (IX). The actual gate of Hell is guarded only by the inscription that opens Canto III, though the inscription takes the form of an elaborate prosopopeia that turns the gate itself into a kind of guardian personification: *"Per me* si va ne la città dolente,"* and so on (emphasis added). For these episodes see *The Divine Comedy,* trans. Charles S. Singleton, I, *Inferno* (Princeton: Princeton University Press, 1970), pt. 1, 46–47, 58–61, 67–69, 90–93, 24–25, respectively.

30. *The Twickenham Edition of the Poems of Alexander Pope,* I, ed. E. Audra and Aubrey Williams (New Haven: Yale University Press, 1961), 192–193; V, ed. James Sutherland, 3rd ed. (1963), 407–409.

31. The resemblance between Gray's ode and "Yew-Trees" is pointed out by Hartman, "Use and Abuse," p. 171.

32. *The Poems of Thomas Gray, William Collins, and Oliver Goldsmith,* ed. Roger Lonsdale (London: Longman, 1969), pp. 60–63. Lonsdale, who traces the passage to Virgil, also mentions several personification clusters not discussed here: descriptions of the Temple of Mars in Statius' *Thebaid,* Chaucer's *Knight's Tale,* and Dryden's *Palamon and Arcite;* and an account of the destructive passions in Thomson's *Spring* (60–61n).

33. One critic has attempted to read the poem in terms of Mircea Eliade's accounts of the difference between sacred and profane spaces; see Gene W. Ruoff, "Wordsworth's 'Yew-trees' and Romantic Perception," *Modern Language Quarterly,* 34 (1973), 146–160. Despite its resemblance to a temple, however, the grove seems curiously empty of sacred attributes.

34. Riffaterre, "Interpretation and Descriptive Poetry," pp. 252, 251.

Epilogue

1. For a summary of the iconographic material, see Fowler's commentary in *The Poems of John Milton,* ed. John Carey and Alastair Fowler (London: Longman, 1968), pp. 690–691n. Fowler relies in part on the foremost scholar of Milton's similes, James Whaler, who unhesitatingly treats the passage as a simile rather than a literal metamorphosis in "Animal Simile in *Paradise Lost,*" *PMLA,* 47 (1932), 544–545.

2. *"Paradise Lost" and the Seventeenth Century Reader* (1947; rpt. Ann Arbor: University of Michigan Press, 1967), p. 50.

3. Anne Davidson Ferry, *Milton's Epic Voice: The Narrator in "Paradise Lost"* (Cambridge, Mass.: Harvard University Press, 1963), pp. 131–132. For remarks on "the crude mechanistic existence of allegorical being" in the Sin and Death episodes, see Arnold Stein, *Answerable Style: Essays on "Paradise Lost"* (Seattle: University of Washington Press, 1953), pp. 157–158. J. B. Broadbent, who otherwise criticizes the allegory as harshly as Johnson does, nevertheless agrees with Stein and Ferry that "Sin and Death are shadowy and temporary figures because they are, ultimately, unreal—figments of the 'evil imagination' " (*Some Graver Subject: An Essay on "Paradise Lost,"* 1960; rpt. New York: Schocken, 1967, pp. 128–129).

4. William Empson, *Milton's God,* rev. ed. (1965; rpt. Cambridge: Cambridge University Press, 1981), p. 279n.

5. See Gallagher's entire essay " 'Real or Allegoric': The Ontology of Sin and Death in *Paradise Lost,*" *English Literary Renaissance,* 6 (1976), 317–335. The quoted remarks appear on pp. 317, 318, 323.

6. Gallagher, "Real or Allegoric," p. 325. He goes on, in fact, to endorse Ferry's view that allegory is specially appropriate to the representation of evil.

7. Empson wryly complains that "the episode of Sin . . . makes the biology of the angels too hard to get clear" (*Milton's God,* p. 59). The allegorical terms are provided by the New Testament: "Then when lust hath conceived, it bringeth forth sin: and sin, when it is finished, bringeth forth death" (James 1:15).

8. Every previous agent except, perhaps, Mammon, who is ludicrously depicted as enamored of precious metals even before his fall (I.679–684):

> *Mammon,* the least erected Spirit that fell
> From Heav'n, for ev'n in Heav'n his looks and thoughts
> Were always downward bent, admiring more
> The riches of Heav'n's pavement, trodd'n Gold,
> Than aught divine or holy else enjoy'd
> In vision beatific . . .

Milton's literal demonology, according to which classical and Near Eastern deities were really bad angels in disguise, hardly requires that the demons actually share the specific vices they assume for the sake of tempting mortals. Since Mammon reappears in a far more dignified role in book II, Milton's treatment of him seems another instance of a single agent oscillating between a literal and a figurative status.

9. Joseph H. Summers, *The Muse's Method: An Introduction to "Paradise Lost"* (Cambridge, Mass.: Harvard University Press, 1962), pp. 49, 50.

10. For a lucid summary of the relevant tendencies in attitudes toward language, see Stanley Eugene Fish, *Surprised by Sin: The Reader in "Paradise Lost,"* 2nd ed. (Berkeley: University of California Press, 1971), pp. 107–127. According to William G. Madsen, Milton, in *Christian Doctrine,* "evidences the same cautious, rationalistic approach to metaphor that Bacon, Hobbes, and the proponents of the Royal Society do" (*From Shadowy Types to Truth: Studies in Milton's Symbolism,* New Haven: Yale University Press, 1968, p. 70). On Milton's conservative and literal-minded attitude toward Scripture, see H. R. MacCallum's indispensable article "Milton and Figurative Interpretation of the Bible," *University of Toronto Quarterly,* 31 (1961–1962), 397–415.

11. Mazzoni and Phillips were long ago cited in this connection by Ida Langdon in *Milton's Theory of Poetry and Fine Art* (New Haven: Yale University Press, 1924), pp. 148–150.

12. I am indebted to Catherine Gallagher for phrasing the latter alternative.

13. For a recent critique of the assumptions underlying most versions of epistemology since the seventeenth century, see Richard Rorty, *Philosophy and the Mirror of Nature* (Princeton: Princeton University Press, 1979). Wilfred Cantwell Smith traces the development of an epistemologically specialized notion of "belief" in *Belief and History* (Charlottesville: University Press of Virginia, 1977). For the effect of epistemological tendencies on the interpretation of Scripture, see Hans W. Frei, *The Eclipse of Biblical Narrative: A Study in Eighteenth and Nineteenth Century Hermeneutics* (New Haven: Yale University Press, 1974).

The tendency to identify the philosophical issue of belief with the political and religious problem of enthusiasm is visible in numerous texts. The clearest example is perhaps Locke's brief chapter "Of Enthusiasm," added to the fourth edition of his central work (1700); see *An Essay Concerning Human Understanding,* ed. Peter H. Nidditch (Oxford: Clarendon, 1975), pp. 697–706.

14. The precise role of Lockean empiricism in eighteenth-century and Romantic aesthetics is subject to disagreement. The standard view—that the Romantics rebelled against the eighteenth century's infatuation with Lockean dualism—meets an eloquent challenge in Ernest Tuveson, *The Imagination as a Means of Grace: Locke and the Aesthetics of Romanticism* (Berkeley: University of California Press, 1960). My own view, implicit in the account of Coleridge in Chapter 1, is that Romantic gestures toward idealism amount to a further development of the eighteenth-century ambivalence toward belief, and thus remain essentially consonant with Lockean attitudes.

15. I use the expression "liberal thought" in the broad sense developed by Roberto M. Unger in his remarkable essay *Knowledge and Politics* (New York: Free Press–Macmillan, 1975).

Index

Abrams, M. H., 1, 45, 56
Addison, Joseph, 140, 141; ambivalence toward allegory, 82; on "fiction," 156n10; on Milton's Sin and Death, 2, 52, 53–58, 62; on personification, 53–54, 57–61, 62, 63
Aeschylus, 63, 95
Allegory: ambivalence toward, 1–2, 5, 42, 48, 82, 87, 149n7; Coleridge on, 10–17, 24–25, 30, 35–36, 83–84, 133, 149n7, 150nn11,14, 150–151n16, 152n28; as oscillation, 48; in painting vs. in poetry, 60–61, 158–159n30; vs. symbol, 1, 14–25, 30, 150n14, 150–151n16. *See also* Personification; Sin and Death, Milton's allegory of
Allegory of Sin and Death. *See* Sin and Death, Milton's allegory of
Ambivalence: toward allegory/personification, 1–2, 5, 42, 48, 52, 82, 87, 140, 149n7; toward archaic belief, 98, 140, 166n59; and Coleridge, 5, 25, 42–44, 48, 79, 106, 149n7; and Collins, 87; and Kant, 3–4, 79, 82, 163n31; and sublime, 3–4, 79, 107, 129, 163n31, 165n50
Ariosto, Lodovico, 54
Aristotle, 56, 64, 71, 92, 94, 148n2, 157n13
Atterbury, Francis, 52
Augustine, Saint, 45, 47
Austin, J. L., 151n20

Bacon, Francis, 6, 172n10
Barbauld, Mrs. A. L., 67
Beattie, James, 121
Belief, 42, 141, 165n50, 172n13; ambivalence toward archaic, 98, 140, 166n59; Coleridge on, 41; and Collins, 97; and Milton's Sin and Death, 55–56, 62, 64. *See also* Empiricism; Self, empirical vs. normative
Bible: Coleridge on, 13–14, 18–19, 20, 22–23, 24, 41–42; Luther on, 40–41; Wordsworth on, 104–105